Buffalo's Occult Architecture

The Spiritual, the Supernatural, and the Niagara's Great Builders

Mason Winfield

RPSS PUBLISHING

RPSS Publishing

429 Englewood Avenue, Kenmore, NY 14223

rpsspublishing.com

publisher@rockpapersafetyscissors.com

978-1-956688-38-2 Buffalo's Occult Architecture - Hardcover

Printed in the USA

RPSS PUBLISHING

"Poetry," Robert Frost once said, "is the sound of the voice intertwined with the words." Architecture, one could say, is the sound of the designer's voice intermingled with his architectural vocabulary. The German philosopher Schelling once observed that architecture is frozen music. Music and poetry being similar, a person could justifiably vary that metaphor to: Architecture is frozen poetry. Both music and literature eschew clumsiness, banality, and cacophony and embrace matters such as theme, inventiveness, harmony, flow, smooth transition, felicitous repetition, appropriate language, and a sense of unity–the same qualities found in good architecture. The traits that make *Hamlet* a masterwork of literature are similar to those that make the Guaranty Building a masterwork of architecture.

– Austin M. Fox

BUFFALO'S OCCULT ARCHITECTURE

INTRODUCTION

SPOOKS AND STRUCTURES

I tell people all the time that I don't know what a ghost is. I can't tell you what makes one appear, and I can't tell you why it would. All I can give you is patterns in the way people tell their accounts. But one thing is for sure: If there's nothing going on with ghosts, it's not been going on for a mighty long time.

Rain forest cultures in the Amazon and the Tropical Andes have their traditions about the reappearance of late ancestors. The classical Japanese told ghost stories. The Romans told ghost stories. The Greeks told ghost stories. One of the classic novels in Chinese tradition is Pu Songling's *Strange Tales from a Chinese Studio*–a collection of old supernatural stories. When the world's shamans went into their trance state they were thought to have entered the realm of the spirits.

Some of the ancient cave paintings in Spain and France are interpreted to represent the concept of a detachable soul or life-essence. No one knows exactly what the Neolithic artists thought, but... A crew of celebrating human hunters flanks a handful of solid-appearing prey animals drawn in charcoal on a cave wall. A stick surely representing the haft of a spear protrudes from the back of the last of them. Above it floats a shadowy representation of the animal, apparently rising to a realm past the earth. If that's not supposed to be a ghost, what is? Believe in them or not, this is a subject that isn't going away. Not as long as people talk.

When somebody tells me they saw a ghost, I don't know what they saw. How could I? I wasn't there at the time of the experience. I am not so much a materialist as to discount the possibility that they could have seen something. Same reason.

Figure: 3

I do know two things. One: Somebody told me a story. Two: where the story happened. (If witnesses decline to tell me the site, I tuck away the laptop or clipboard and tell them to contact me when they are serious.)

I have two constants, then: story and site. Some places pick up stories for centuries. Some get none. You concede that. There are vast stretches of undeveloped landscape and uninspiring cityscapes that get no ghost stories. What castle or battlefield lacks them? What are the similarities between places that get stories? What are the similarities in the way people tell their stories? That's been pretty much my approach for the last twenty years. There are patterns to be found.

As a kid, I was outrageously bored by almost every moment in school. I was a bookworm, though. I read history, yes, but fantasy, mythology, science fiction, horror, and adventure were all on the menu. I read widely on subjects of the paranormal, too–the allegedly "real"

Opposite Page - Figure: 2

Figure: 5

Figure: 4

supernatural. I was well positioned for a leap into research on the subject if I ever chose it.

In the middle 1990s I started work on my first book *Shadows of the Western Door* (1997), a survey of the upstate supernatural/ paranormal, past and present. Despite my long recreational interest, I surely came to the study with most of the preconceptions of every other non-specialist.

I was inclined to think that ghosts were real, if undependable, and that disagreements about their existence were due to nothing more than their general unreliability–and sincere opinions in those who had never seen one. I thought they were manifestations of past events, if not the purposeful spirit-forms of late humans. More complicated situations of psychic phenomena–like poltergeist episodes, possession cases, and religious miracles–I hadn't fully processed. Not ghosts, exactly, they seemed part of the mystery of the world.

I also thought haunted sites would be exceptional. It certainly looked that way when I started out. There were no studies of our region. Only a handful of significant Niagara Frontier buildings had been mentioned in print as haunts. Our supernatural folklore came up in tidbits, and it was generally recorded as an afterthought. It was before the internet and the ghost-hunting boom had hit. It was, frankly, before my regional books were in print.

Some of the old town and county histories made cryptic references to haunted houses, woods, hills, or valleys. Some of those turned out to be good leads, but it took a lot of follow-up to see if any of them could develop into something that would be fun for anyone to read. I had to forage. I had to consult many sources to build a picture about a single site. I had to delve through libraries, visit historians, track witnesses, haul out microfilms, and go through folders of dusty papers, some of them family journals and diaries.

In short, the research for the strong sites–ones with a pedigree, ones with layers of human, historic, and architectural significance and decades of ghostly folklore– was not easy at first. By 2000 it was so easy to list reputed haunts in the upstate that I found myself interested in patterns: the big picture.

———

I spun my first book into a company devoted to "supernatural tourism," Haunted History Ghost Walks, Inc. I led my first ghost walk of East Aurora in 1997. We're still up and running, though by now I have a number of tour guides and a variety of tours of local villages. I also have competition.

I used to lead tours of Buffalo's fabled waterfront, Canalside, in the first two summers of its official opening. Almost all the tales I told about the area were old ones, from before its reconstruction: from prehistory, the frontier period, and the 19th century. I pointed to spaces in earth, water, and brickwork and tried to get people envisioning past events and vanished buildings. I told tales about the waterfront and the Old First Ward. While the public tends to love gripping bloodcurdlers–and most of our tours have a couple–those old ones are my favorites. They're usually the hardest to get, too. For that Canalside tour we had almost nothing but.

Nobody seemed to mind. Yet on one of my bigger tours–there had to be ninety people–a gent who had kept close to me most of the evening pulled me aside. "Why don't we have any stories from, like, now?" he said. He was right. Nothing is left of the original waterfront village. The new builds at the redeveloped Canalside don't seem to be haunted.

"We've lost the buildings," I said on the spot. "When you lose the buildings, you lose the stories." I had never thought about it that way before, but I couldn't have given him a better answer today.

It's still impressive to think of how many of the greatest architects in American tradition are represented in Buffalo. Yet we've lost a lot of great buildings, and we don't seem to have a hold on the cycle. And you lose a lot more than a neat building when you lose some of them. You lose more than stories. You lose a connection to those who came before. Some of the time, you lose mystery.

———

My ghost walks were popular from the start. The research for them got me out into the public, both interviewing witnesses and fielding questions from tour-goers. I got quite a few surprises. I should probably make a top ten list of them someday and deliver it as a lecture, because it's illuminating.

One of the most impactful of those surprises was the realization that, while storied houses were uncommon, they weren't rare. One out of ten in the typical neighborhood would be a high number. One out of a hundred would be low, at least wherever I looked on the Niagara. In some neighborhoods or stretches of street, half the sites were said to be once or currently haunted.

I noticed another pattern: Unless it was a school or hospital, I almost never got a ghost story out of contemporary commercial architecture. One of the few sites that broke the pattern was a strip mall in Fort Erie, ONT, that, as best I can tell, is located on the turf of one of the niftiest frontier forest-fights–if you liked that big jump scene outside Fort George in *Last of the Mohicans* (1992)–of the Niagara war. At least 150 men died in a woodsy bushwhack in July of 1814. Sensing that that might leave some psychic echoes, I got out the old maps, tried to find the onetime wood, and simply went to what was currently there and started asking around, notepad in hand. I got some odd reports from people who worked in these red-brick rectangles, even though none knew they were on battlefield.

I noticed another pattern that took me a long time to process: Almost none of our grand, historic, buildings– government offices, hotels, museums, and churches–were without some kind of ghostly story. Is the fact that a building looks big and spooky all it takes to get people talking about it? Is there nothing like that that isn't haunted? If that's the big picture, what's it all worth?

In short, if a building was constructed on the site of something significant, it could get folklore no matter what it looked like. If it was built in a classic form, it would get stories no matter where it was. Somewhere in there seemed to be a constant. What to make of it?

Obviously, the site and the architecture were the variables.

Figure: 6

I have always cultivated acquaintances with people who could teach me something. If someone had anything interesting to say, even if I didn't agree with it, it never mattered to me where they stood on the social or political spectrum. I would talk to them, sometimes at length. Some of those interesting people became friends. The author and mystic Sig Lonegren is such a figure.

Lefties and dyslexics, they say, tend to be "out of the box" thinkers. I've forgotten which hand he uses, but Sig is surely an original. Sig was a young trustee at The Gow School, an internationally known school for dyslexic youth, when I was a rookie teacher. He was even then a prominent author, and he's forged avenues of new thinking about labyrinths, dyslexia, and dowsing. (Dowsers—"water witches"—are people who find water or other underground peculiarities, usually by using implements— wands, pendulums, L-rods, or forked

Figure: 7

sticks. I say "usually" because the legendary Welsh dowser Bill Lewis was so good by the end of his career that he needed nothing but his open palm to detect "the Force.")

Sig had earned his Master's Degree from the progressive and experimental Goddard College. "Sacred Space" was a design-your-own major, and Sig had been a serious student. Most of our discussions covered the megalithic monuments of the British Isles and Northwestern Europe that had long fascinated me. Sig often called the study, "Sacred Enclosures," since it refers also to outdoor sites and monuments like mounds and stone circles. Sacred Enclosures are human-signified declarations of Sacred Space, acknowledged to be special— to the deities, to the natural forces, the Ancestors, or to the human spirit.

Yet Sacred Space is with us still, and cross-culturally. Sig established mind-blowing connections from the deep

past to the near-present, at least when it came to architecture and the related mathematics. Architecture is a continuum that goes back to its roots. Sacred Space is a human tradition.

Sig was in good shape to comment from another perspective. He had been a member of The Dragon Project, a fascinating, relatively short-lived British-Continental research society most active in the 1970s. The Dragon Project had the mission to subject the old sacred monuments to a rigorous and multi-disciplinary study. It applied the insights of the objective and the subjective— the left and right brain. Monuments were studied not only through hard measurement but also through dream- and ESP experiments. These places, they found, were not just old and sacred. They were special. Many had been built and sited with uncanny precision. Their direct purposes remained mysterious.

Figure: 8

The Dragon Project didn't stop at Bronze Age monuments like Avebury and Stonehenge. They studied sacred buildings of every kind, including little village churches and the grand cathedrals. They found uncanny parallels: of geometry, astronomy, geology, and even alignment. The old-timers had incorporated physical man-made space with earthly and celestial parameters with the goal, almost surely, of enhancing the human religious experience—or should I say, the trance experience. The old-timers would have incorporated all the factors that would have been relevant to them to create this altered state.

Sig talked about mathematical and geometrical codes, earthly energies, astronomical alignments, and symbolic shapes. He also pointed out the continuity that exists between ancient sacred styling and more recent structures. If someone was recreating the old styles of architecture down to a formula, he or she was creating Sacred Space, at least geometrically.

"If you got one of the classic architects around the turn of the century to build your house," said my friend,

10

"whether you know it or not, you're living in a little church."

My eyes must have glazed over as I processed that. "You know, another thing about those old sacred spaces," he said. "They pick up a lot of ghost stories."

———

Figure: 9

So marked was this connection between classic architecture and ghost stories that I began to look for it as a pattern. I talked about it at lectures and on tours. I didn't publish much about it. The connection hadn't made its way into the ghost-business, and I didn't mind keeping it that way. This understanding and the ability to explicate it was one of the real hooks to my company's tours. I didn't want to hand my competitors a handbook.

In 2009 I was writing a book on the supernatural folklore of Saratoga Springs, NY, and had some questions about the village architecture. One of my main resources was a book by a living author–retired professor James Kettlewell. On a Saturday afternoon I cold-called him and asked my questions about village building styles and architects.

I found Professor Kettlewell to be the model of the scholar: welcoming, well informed about a wide variety of subjects, and as good as anyone you can get. By the end we were getting along so well that I decided to spring it on him. "You know, Professor," I said, "there's a connection between architecture and ghost stories."

Every architect comes across generalized talk about haunted sites. Few, including Professor Kettlewell, take much interest in it. The professor is traditional. The paranormal is "out there." He seemed flustered, even ready to be affronted. "What… What do you mean?"

I developed for him in two sentences what I've developed for you so far: the old styles, Gothic, neoclassical, Egyptianate, Mayan Revival, Italianate, Romanesque… These are where you get all the stories. Commercial architecture: strip malls, McDonald's, Rite-Aid… No stories. You could hear him thinking.

Then he spoke. *Oh, my God, you're right!*

I am. Why would there be a connection between classic architecture and supernatural folklore? Why would ancient churchy architecture be perpetuated by postindustrial architects, anyway?

SACRED SPACE

In the preindustrial world, you could build your house or your barn just about any way you wanted. The job was to get it to stand up and then use it. This would be what you'd call, "vernacular architecture." It's not designed by an architect. It's constructed. It's been estimated that 95% of the world's buildings are of this type: made to no particular philosophy or with any other purpose but utility. They also call this, "folk architecture."

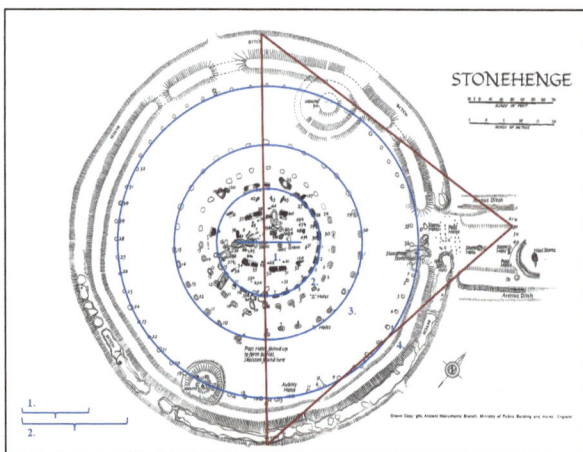

Figure: 11

Things were different if a building was important to a whole cultural group, particularly one whose state was not too far separated from its church. There you got the designers out. Preindustrial cultures of any development reserved special parameters for their important buildings: temples, political structures, and palaces. All over the world this was so. The inclination to what we call "sacred architecture" seems to be a common human impulse.

The specifics of shape, proportion, siting, and alignment were not identical across the world. The factors tended to run in cultural spheres, though they could have some impressive long-range and cross-cultural correlations. There are similarities in geometry–though not in appearance–between Britain's Stonehenge, Egypt's Great Pyramid, and many a grand Christian cathedral. Look at the Great Pyramid's profile set atop Stonehenge.

I look at this less as proof of Atlantis or ET's than as evidence of a shared cultural source or something a wide range of humans have perceived to be similar about the

world. If nothing else, it illustrates the fact that architecture is a continuum, to an extent that would shock most of you.

Closer to the present, it becomes a revivalist trend to use the parameters of the old temples. Yet they are perpetuated, and many of Buffalo's prominent architects maintained them.

———

"Classic sacred architecture," Sig Lonegren told me once, "involves sacred geometry, archaeoastronomy, and sacred geology." I would add a fourth component, "sacred alignment." Let's discuss them.

SACRED GEOMETRY

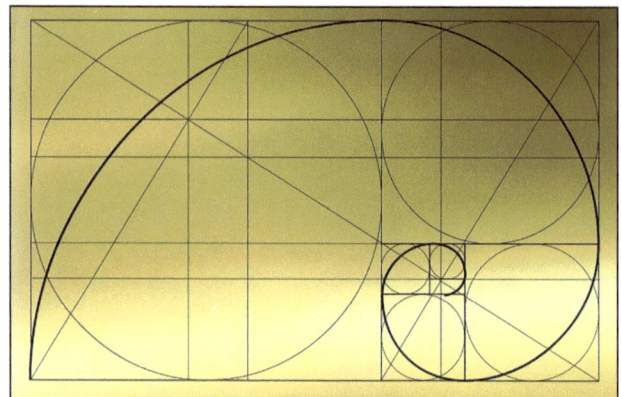

Figure: 12

The most obvious component of sacred architecture is using certain proportions and shapes for a building's structure. This you can see, though not always recognize. These forms and ratios can be expressed in very subtle ways. Some of this you might even regard as "fractal": shapes repeated almost as themes in a variety of sizes.

In the West the base form tends to be the Golden Section or -Rectangle, but this unique shape has a lot of spins, including special triangles, arcs, pentagons, pentagrams, and a very precise spiral. We've included an image suggesting some of the curiosities in this graceful form.

The Golden Rectangle is built out of a square. A

Opposite Page - Figure: 13

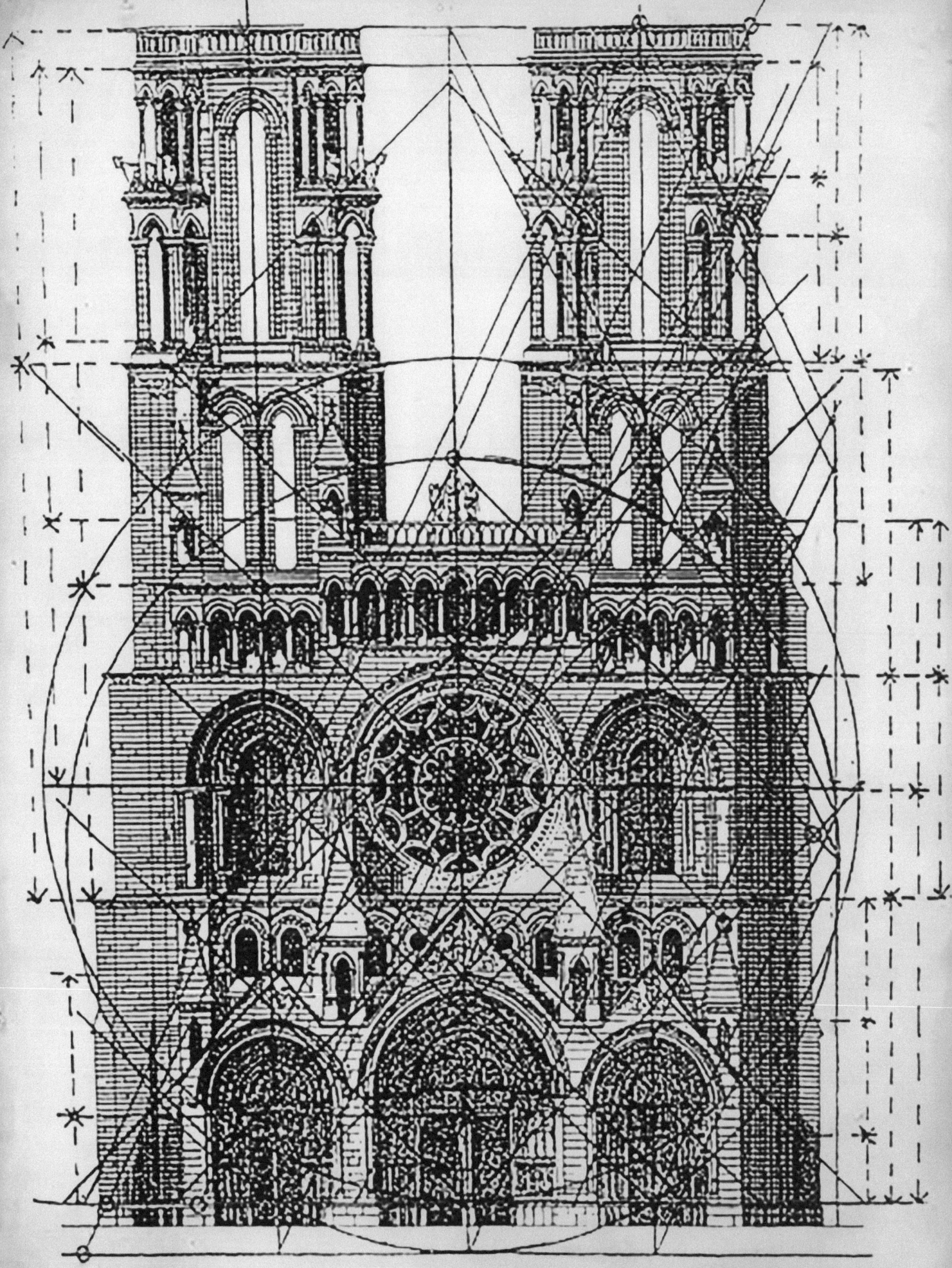

CATEDRAL DE LAON (M. LUND)

rectangle whose long side is equal in length to a side of the square is tacked onto it. The short side of that rectangle must be .618... of the side of the square. They call this the phi ("fee") ratio. It's as infinite and incalculable as pi. Just keeps going.

That will make the big new rectangle the same exact shape as the one you just tacked on. That's one of the miracles of this form. The Golden Rectangle is regarded as a very pleasing shape, too. It's the backbone of Greek artistic and architectural philosophy–and that of anyone it

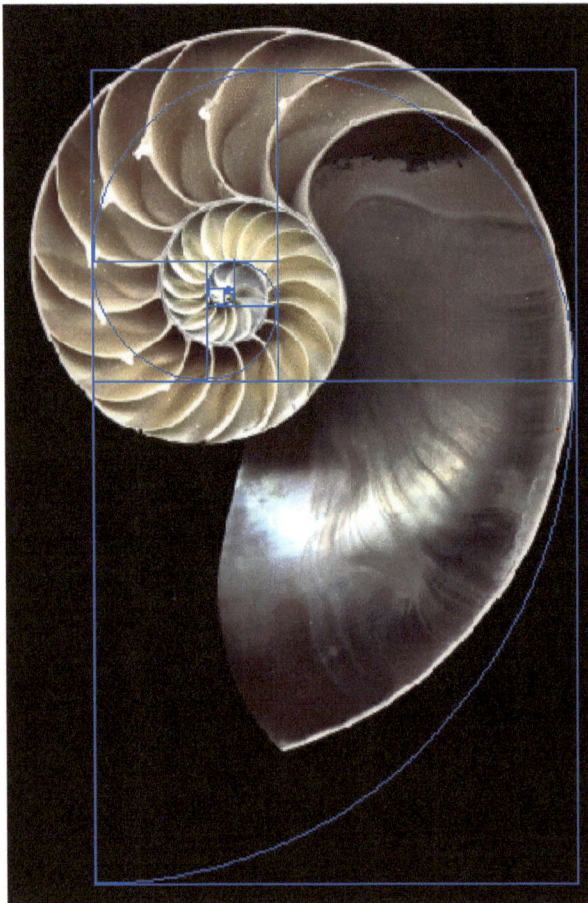

Figure: 14

influenced. Most of us unconsciously like looking at things in that shape. The faces of most of your "beautiful people" correspond with the Golden Rectangle.

While we get our impressions of the Golden Section/Ratio/Rectangle through classic Greek tradition and their imitators in Rome and, later, the rest of Europe, I've heard that its real root may be with the Egyptians. It's become an important form in the visual arts and architecture. It's out there in the world, especially that spiral that derives from it.

For astronomers, that spiral is in the equation for a galaxy.

In biology, it's the growth curve of a nautilus shell.

In botany, it's the seed pattern of a sunflower, a pineapple, an apple, and a pine cone.

In geometry, it's the ratio of the diagonal of a pentagon to its side.

For stock brokers, it's the basis for the wave principle of the market's fluctuations.

For crystallographers, it's the ratio of the terraces in aluminum-copper-iron alloys.

For musicians, it's in the shape of a Stradivarius violin.

In number theory, it's the famous Fibonacci series and all its permutations.

In popular film and fiction, it's at the heart of Dan Brown's *The Da Vinci Code*.

For mathematicians, the ratio behind it is simply the most beautiful irrational number there is.

Clearly, the Rectangle and the forms that spin off of it are representations of universal forces. The Greeks were onto something.

There's an occasionally heated debate about the direct use of the Golden Section in Greek and Roman architecture. To say that all classical buildings evoke this shape would be as incorrect as to say that few of them did. It was the signature form for classical architecture.

I can't tell just by eyeballing a building if it's been wrought with sacred shape. It's usually a lot more involved than simply a footprint or facade. The giveaway may be that sacred architecture "just looks cool." Even small buildings wrought in the classic forms are often unaccountably charming to the eye. But where you can get the plans of a building–or a good square-on photograph–you can start to get the hint. We'll show you that in Buffalo a few times in this book.

The Golden Section permeates Western sacred architecture. "These concepts were, to the ancients, not merely mathematics, but were infused with spiritual meaning," writes Will Selman. "Universal truths were to be found in their understanding." That included not only for the artist or architect, but the general public who were

ONE UNIT TIMES 1.618

DEN MEAN ERMINES SZE LINE

ONE UNIT

GEORGIAN STYLE HOUSE
WITH FRONT ELEVATION

ONE UNIT TIMES 1.618

Figure: 15

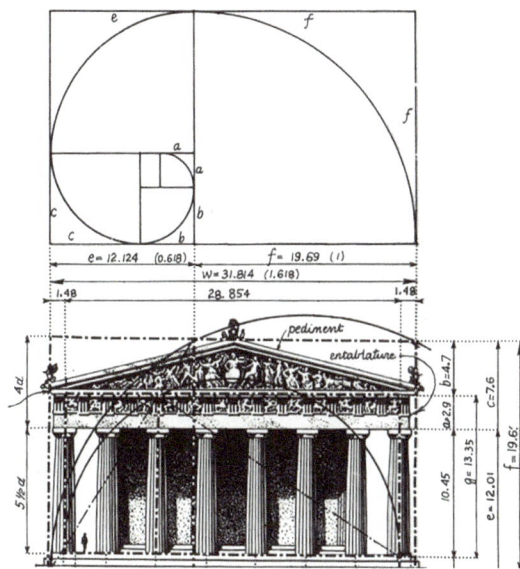

Figure: 16

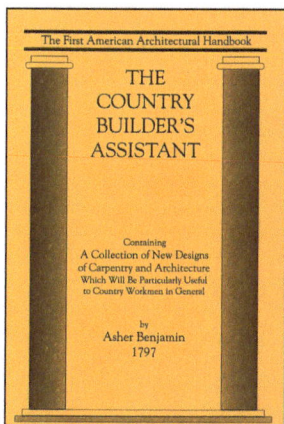

Figure: 17

merely exposed to these building types.

The appearance of the Golden Section and other Greek features on an old Niagara building could be a mixed message. In a Greek revival farmhouse it could have been because most of those were made or adapted from a relatively small number of patterns. Don't forget that in the early years of our Union, there was almost no professional designer class. People didn't use architects. They built their own houses. In 1797 Asher Benjamin (1773-1845) published the classic, *The Country Builder's Assistant*. Minard Lafever (1798-1854) followed with *The Young Builders' General Instructor* (1829). Companies like Sears cut, packaged, and delivered wood in kits–with handbooks! The plans were all neoclassical. That's why you see so many little wooden Greek temples–columned porches and pediments–tacked onto boxy houses on those old lanes around Western New York.

Greek architecture was popular in the post-Revolutionary United States because of an admiration for Greek culture, as well as a resentment against anything British. This was ironic, since Britain and most of the rest of the West was well into its neoclassical–"copy the Greeks and Romans"–kick.

The Golden Shape was a favored form for Frank Lloyd Wright. The Golden Spiral was the base design of his Guggenheim Museum in New York. We'll see that H. H. Richardson evoked it but modified it, and completely with intention–like adding an extra square or rectangle to the base form and using it for a building's theme. We'll see that Louis Sullivan used the form for his one Buffalo building. With the classicists to come in E. B. Green and E. E. Joralemon, the frequent use should be presumed. The Golden Ratio may underlie the work of every architect in this book, for that matter. The reason we don't know it may be that others are less studied–or less obvious about it.

Yet other shapes are prominent in sacred architecture. The double-square (or cube) may be the most common of them. It was one of the major shapes for the medieval Knights Templar–another potential founding influence for the Freemasons. Sig Lonegren told me that the Shakers and possibly the Quakers were quite fond of the double-square as a form for their meeting houses.

The use of the flat-topped ("unfinished") pyramid has to be suspected as a tribute to Egyptianism, which is one of the gestures of sacred architecture and an expression of a Masonic or Rosicrucian interest. I interpret the top of the very curious tower at East Aurora's Roycroft Inn to be so, not just because it looks that way but because it is one of a number of

Figure: 18

Egyptianate features at that worthy Campus. This tower includes Golden Rectangle proportioning, with suggestions of other intrigues.

The Vesica Piscis is a curvier form made by two overlapping circles of identical size whose perimeters come to rest on each other's center points. That eye-shaped fish-body, "the lens," in the middle is a medieval symbol you see a lot in the arches and windows of Gothic cathedrals. The Freemasons use the form as well.

Figure: 19a and 19b

The octagon is another popular form in Western sacred architecture, design, and philosophy. Also a key figure of Asian thought and landscape design, the regular octagon is fairly common, too, in Native North American sacred landscape architecture. The octagon became a 19th century fad in the United States, which deserves a special aside because two Western New Yorkers, Orson and Lorenzo Fowler, almost single-handedly launched the revival. With Lorenzo's wife Lydia, the Fowlers became famous as proponents of phrenology–skull-reading–one of the age's prominent pseudo-sciences. Phrenology took them on a lot of tangents, including the advocacy of the octagonal form in house-building. I don't know of one octagonal house in Western New York that lacks a few ghost stories.

The octagon was also one of the few occult shapes medieval Christianity seemed to like. The octagon and the octogram, the eight-pointed star, were religious symbols because the eight-sided form symbolizes renewal, rebirth, regeneration, and transition. The octagon shape was the focus of a trend in 19th century Western architecture. Western New York, indeed–"the Burned-over District"–

Figure: 20

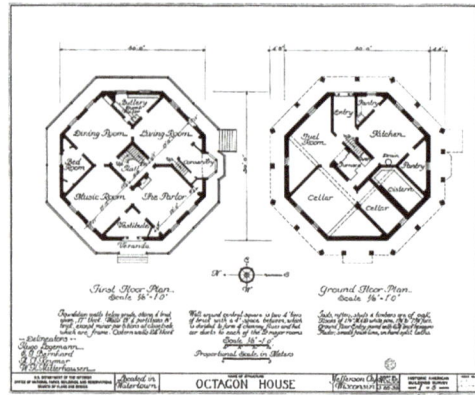

Figure: 21

was a focus for the octagon house. The West's prime Classical architect, Vitruvius, was a fan of the octagonal form. He advocated whole cities being designed around it.

While there is debate about the extent of the use of a form called "the Egyptian triangle" by the people who built the pyramids, the appearance of the shape in fairly recent architecture could be considered another tribute to Egyptianism and sacred design. This triangle is alleged to be a diagonal cross-section of the Great Pyramid at Giza, hence a spin off the Golden Shape. The Egyptian triangle is the 3-4-5 Pythagorean triangle, and it has other names yet.

 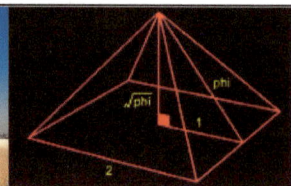

Figure: 22   *Figure: 23*

SACRED ASTRONOMY

The most important preindustrial sacred sites tend to be aligned to astronomical features. Either within its own structure or its positioning with other sites, a sacred enclosure can point to lines of progress of heavenly bodies or to manifestations of them–rises, sets, or zeniths–on special dates. The most common points of alignment worldwide are either to the four compass directions or the solstices.

Monuments in the Americas were trickier. Some made statements with local natural features. One of the pyramids at Teotihuacan, for instance, is thought to honor a mountain on the horizon. The Hopewell cultures of the

Opposite Page - Figure: 24

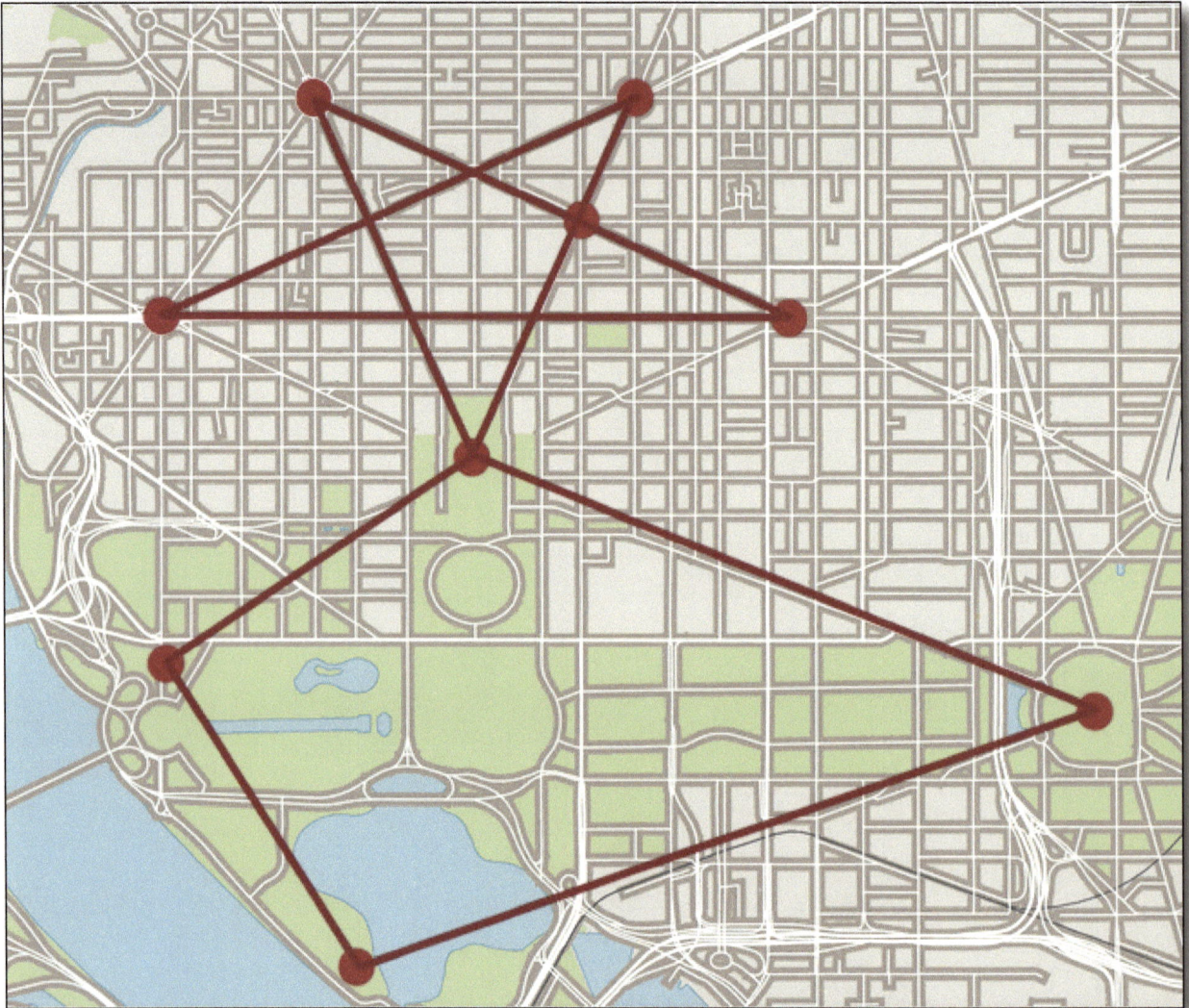

Mississippi and Ohio valleys seemed to like more unique astronomical events like moonrises and -sets. Others honored culturally-significant calendar dates. Some Maya societies seemed fascinated with the planet Venus, and some of their structures marked its movements. Upstate

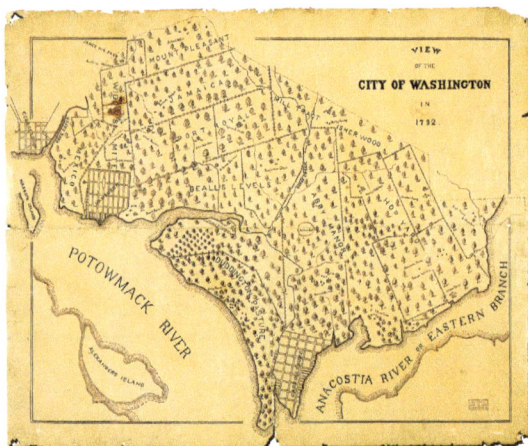

Figure: 25

New York had its ancient monuments, too, though it's lost most of them. I would expect them to have made their messages, though I'd think we've lost the chance to crack whatever code they expressed.

Archaeoastronomy is not thought to be one of the reflexes of postindustrial city planners, and I wouldn't expect to find it much in today's Buffalo. It's harder for postindustrial architects, too. Bronze Age priesthoods and medieval kings had a lot of control over their sites. In the postindustrial world even for a Wright or a Richardson, the footprint of a site was usually marked. (Here's the lot. Here's the budget. What can you fit into it for us?)

Archaeoastronomy does exist with us, though. People who have preserved other traditions of the ancient world, like the Freemasons, believed in alignment across landscape. Just take a look at the base plan of Washington, DC.

18

Where I know of archaeoastronomy in any of our Buffalo structures I'll report it, but it's beyond my expertise to detect it. I'm lucky to be able to spell it.

SACRED GEOLOGY

This subject is controversial. I don't feel confident in all the points made by the most devout advocates. Much as I respect the discipline of dowsing, I need more than the word of a "water witch" to tell you that underground water sources like blind springs truly underlie dead-center of Stonehenge or key components of some of the grand cathedrals–like altars or confessionals.

It is agreed that the Great Pyramid in Egypt and the Pyramid of the Sun at Teotihuacan were sited over caves; that the Oracle of Delphi had her temple at a natural gas well; and that the sites of many contemporary Marian apparitions–like Lourdes, La Salette, and Fatima–are natural fountains.

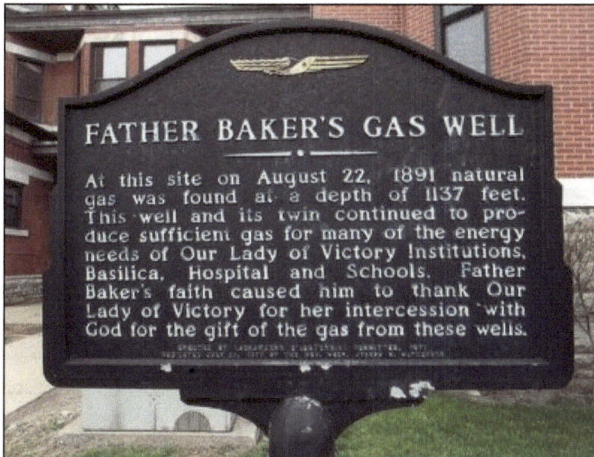

FATHER BAKER'S GAS WELL

At this site on August 22, 1891 natural gas was found at a depth of 1137 feet. This well and its twin continued to produce sufficient gas for many of the energy needs of Our Lady of Victory Institutions, Basilica, Hospital and Schools. Father Baker's faith caused him to thank Our Lady of Victory for her intercession with God for the gift of the gas from these wells.

Figure: 27

It's also known that Father Baker's basilica complex in Lackawanna, NY, is rooted around a deep gas well whose location the someday-saint detected with sheer vision. A handful of dowsers tell us that the power-tower of East Aurora's Roycroft Inn is over a blind spring. The shrine of the Mohawk saint Kateri in Fonda, NY, is by a spring. And you can't find a building on the east side of Broadway Avenue in Saratoga Springs–on the fault–that lacks a ghost story.

Here's one thing that isn't controversial: Wherever there is a break in the earth's crust–a fault, a cave, a gas well, a spring–there's a different energy coming up. A geologist would tell you this. It can be measured. Because of the startling localization of reports of psychic phenomena within the typical allegedly haunted building, I have long wondered if there could be a geological component to a haunting–or a visionary experience.

SACRED ALIGNMENT

This is my contribution, and it should not be controversial. Sacred alignments exist. Most people call these straight,

THE OLD STRAIGHT TRACK
Its Mounds, Beacons, Moats, Sites and Mark Stones
ALFRED WATKINS

Figure: 28   *Figure: 29*

imaginary trails across landscape "ley lines," or the more precise term, "leys," since a ley implies a line. Here we have to be cautious. Since many readers will not know this term, I should elaborate.

In the summer of 1921 the British photographer, antiquarian, and beer salesman Alfred Watkins (1855-1935) had his stunning vision of church steeples, hilltop henges, and standing stones receding into the landscape in perfect alignment. The experience turned into a book–*The Old Straight Track* (1925)–that led to a new way of looking at landscape, as well as a crew of devotees.

Since then, people have thought of leys in three fashions:

–Pathways, ceremonial walking trails connecting sacred/powerful sites

–Lines of force, meridians, along the surface of the earth that sensitive people marked by dotting them with sacred structures

–Imaginary straight line connectors between sacred sites–"places of ancient sanctity," according to the author and paranormalist John Michell. I believe the standard of acceptance for any single ley is still six sites within ten miles.

Few leys make logical or even decent pathways. They shoot across creeks and straight over ravines. No

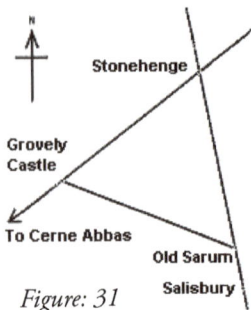

Figure: 30

one's been able to prove the existence of physical energy along any ley, either. The only definition of a ley I can accept is the last one: the imaginary connector. But I believe leys exist. I can't, in fact, understand why anyone would still argue about them. Some preindustrial cultures set up their sacred sites to align with other sacred sites, often those of other cultures.

Native societies in the Americas seem particularly fond of leys. In Ohio, a 60-mile straight connector between two suspiciously similar Hopewell earthworks, one in Newark and one in Chillicothe, seems indisputable.

The Maya cities were joined by straight-line roads of crushed chalk called *sacbeob*, often across many miles. Something often called "The Great Triangle of England" is a six-miles-on-a-side isosceles triangle rooted at Stonehenge and two other once-prominent sacred sites. Also called, "Lockyer's Triangle," its lanes could have been pathways.

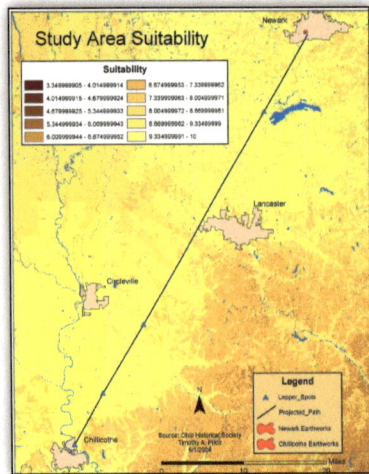

Figure: 31

It seems as though leys have occasionally been brought into the pattern for more contemporary cities. Buffalo has one definite ley that we will speak about later. I think a significant variant of a ley might be an established street or trackway that makes an astronomical message. Washington, DC, has a few of those. Otherwise, I don't expect many leys in North American cities.

Geology, geometry, astronomy… So why would the old-timers go to so much trouble to make their temples? I think you have to look at the point of the religion-business. It starts out as an expression of a collective need in the human psyche. If we don't have God or some sort of ethereal presence to turn to, we'll go for something else. Be careful who you take for your leaders. The 20th century has some bad models.

Once a faith gets established, one of its goals is to keep converts and make more. The old-timers built their churches at least partly to be places that would inspire the trance-state–the visionary state.

In the ancient world, people bought in. You did your church this way because that's how the gods liked it, and your church became one of those "liminal spaces" at which the bounds of the other world and this one were likelier to overlap. Shape, proportion, and positioning were thought to contribute to the thinning of the veil.

Why did the old-timers get the impression that "the gods" liked things along certain patterns? The simple answer is that they observed those patterns in the natural world, the one "the gods" made. I know a Greek temple doesn't look much like a tree, but we've seen that the underlying ratios and shapes–Golden spirals, rectangles, triangles and the rest–are everywhere in the natural world.

In our day, you don't have to believe in the point of sacred architecture to be perpetuating it. All you have to do is follow a style.

———

So why is antique sacred architecture common at all among the work of fairly recent architects? And in Buffalo? There may be two answers.

With the first of them, you have to look at the period. The age of most of Buffalo's primo architecture was the end of a long fad: neoclassicism.

Since 1648 the École des Beaux-Arts has maintained several academies in France that trained many of the world's great painters, sculptors, and architects. The style known as Beaux-Arts was neoclassical: modeled on Greek and Roman forms and proportions. It was a philosophy to

the Beaux-Arts to pass the style on to future generations. They thought it was ennobling to the human spirit to have these beautiful structures to enter and regard. Neoclassicism was a massive fad for centuries in all the arts.

The École had a big influence on architecture in the United States. The École had sympathetic branches in the United States, such as The Beaux-Arts Institute of Design, an art and architectural school in New York City. Anyone who had been so trained had classical styling drummed into them. "The sense of highly organized architecture with a sense of proportion was instilled there," noted Richard Chafee. Thomas Jefferson, a classicist and a great influencer, had a hand in bringing classical architecture to the United States, too. Sacred geometry became a mental template. Even for those rebels like the nation's (and Buffalo's) big three—H. H. Richardson, Louis Sullivan, and Frank Lloyd Wright—the spirit of classicism was not exorcized. It was given new and more subtle dress. Even the Gothic revival and "Richardsonian Romanesque" had elements of classical geometry and symmetry.

Of course, there was a furious rebellion against neoclassicism that overtook the different arts at different periods. The major one in Western painting, drama, and poetry we call *Romanticism*. It got started in the late 1700s and lasted around four decades. In Romantic literary and visual art you can see classical patterns combined with a new emotion, inclusiveness, and ingenuity. The Romantic Age never had its true flowering in architecture, unless you consider the Gothic revival trend to be a backdated Romanticism. I'm not sure it isn't. The Romantic age was indeed that of the Gothic novel.

It took a lot longer for classicism to work itself out in architecture. Though it all, these temple-like formulas were getting recycled. Which brings us to our second reason to see so much sacred architecture in Buffalo.

———

It's not just ancient priesthoods, classical imitators, and revivalist architects who get interested in sacred architecture. There is a big connection between occult ("underground") groups and architecture. That was another of my big surprises when I turned to this study. Why in the world would there be an overlap between architecture and occultism? Why would a mystic make a statement in a building?

First of all, there is nothing implicitly sinister about the word *occult*. It doesn't mean "evil" or "Satanic." It means only something hidden, underground, or for specialists. It means "out of the notice of the mainstream." For the average person, occult disciplines and philosophies are either too much work or not interesting enough.

When you see how complex the philosophies of sacred geometry are and how intricate it is putting them into practice, you see that sacred architecture is not for the mainstream in any age. It's known that the medieval cathedrals were designed and overseen by networks of traveling experts—the rocket scientists of their age.

Empires fall, and styles change. These insiders had to go somewhere once there was no need of their services. Possibly they were so inspired by their studies that they didn't want the world to lose them. They may have survived, merely changing form and name. They may have become some of our contemporary societies, like the original Freemasons.

The Masons do indeed take architecture as their base motif. You can expect at least gestures of sacred architecture to be displayed in any building the Freemasons make for themselves. Anyone interested in Freemasonry or its Greek/Egyptian/Judaic contributing sources will be likely to show the influence in both form and ornament. Some of the cults, alternative religions, and private societies of the West have kept an interest in sacred architecture, too.

The Western pipeline of mystical symbolism and

philosophy is called "the Hermetic-Cabalist tradition." It's the symbol-rich garden of forms and ideas from which most Western occult groups take inspiration. That's why their buzzwords and imagery can overlap.

By now even many churches have stopped bothering with sacred architecture. We've been in the era of declining faith for centuries. I admit that, at least in the details, most religions do make for a tall story. We still have buildings built with sacred architecture, many more than most of us think. The old patterns are still with us. There's no reason to suspect that whatever impact they might have had on us would have changed.

––––––

The British paranormalist Paul Devereux has come up with the term "Exceptional Human Experience" to describe paranormal reports. (Hereafter it's EHE.) This is a clever definition, one that sums what it defines but does not presume to know the cause. Devereux also takes account of the curious clustering effect of supernatural folklore and reported paranormal experience.

Large sites or regions seem to exist at which nearly all manner of paranormal phenomena are storied or reported. We don't just mean ghosts. Mystery-critters, phantom lights, energy-anomalies, occult societies, geological and gravitational abnormalities, human disappearances, supernatural beings, time-lapses, UFOs and related phenomena, and just about any other effect you can think of might be storied or reported in these "paranormal

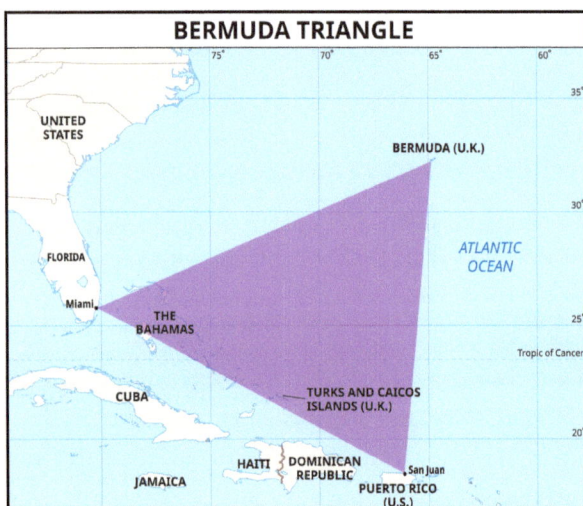

Figure: 34

zones." I won't speculate here on what that says about either human consciousness or those zones themselves.

Some paranormal zones are vast and famous. The Bermuda Triangle and Mt. Shasta are examples. Western New York has a number of sites like these, too, hills, valleys, roads, and even water-bodies that collect all manner of rumor. So far most are only locally famous, though we do have a zone of mystery called "The Great Lakes Triangle."

Some paranormal zones are grand and human-made–sacred enclosures like The Great Pyramid and Stonehenge. A haunted house is a little one.

––––––

So why would the physical form of a building have any effect on people? I remind you of not only the ancient reverence for geometric form but also the 1970s' pop faith in "Pyramid Power." While I agree that Pyramid Power may not have much to back it up, it cannot be denied that some people have maintained the theory that a building's form could influence the human experience within it, physically and otherwise.

So why would a building designed with old temple architecture be more likely to get ghost stories? I have two answers, not mutually exclusive.

1) *Because they look like they ought to be haunted.* There's surely a good likelihood that sites that simply look like ones associated with ghost stories will fire the imagination and get people talking. Folklore, like gossip, can take on its own momentum. That leads us to other questions, though: Why were certain building styles associated with ghost stories in the first place? Because

Figure: 33

22

they were likely to be haunted? Because they were built with sacred architecture?

2) *Because they are haunted.* Or at least they produce some energy that causes people to believe they see things. That, too, bears a short discussion.

I've told you about some of the wonderful teachers in my life. Another of them was Father Alphonsus Trabold (1925-2005), the Franciscan friar and St. Bonaventure University's beloved theology professor.

"Father Al" as he liked to be called would have been the exorcist of the diocese and probably all of Western New York had he ever seen the need to perform a formal–he called it "solemn"–exorcism. He had studied a number of local cases, including the notorious Dandy House in Hinsdale, but he never believed any of the ones brought before him met the standards of being pronounced a true case of "spirit possession."

He was no materialist, though. He believed in hauntings. He believed so implicitly in the other world

Figure: 35

that at least, in his presence, there was no doubt in me. In one of our conversations he conjectured that for all we knew, every square foot of our world could be populated with spirits. Psychic activity manifested only where it could–where there was some power source to hitch on to. That is physics, you know. Even for "the spirits," any effect of force that appears in our world has to have a physical cause. While this power-source could be electrical–since so many poltergeist cases feature actups in human-made devices–it could also be site-based. There is naturally-occurring electrical energy in the air and the earth.

The ancients believed that factors in the siting, orientation, and shape of a building could influence human experience. Could there be a factor like that in our "classic" buildings, even young ones?

————

A few words about supernatural folklore and its more contemporary cousin, paranormal literature and perceived experience. One of its elementals is that we are within the realm of the indefinite–as with the arts. Tidy boundaries do not apply. Without that appreciation, neither subject will make any sense to the objective-minded newcomer.

I turn again to Paul Devereux, one of the pioneers in the understanding of several major paranormal topics. Devereux thinks about paranormal zones like UFO-plagued valleys and legend-rich ancient monuments the way I have started to about haunted houses. They are wonder-zones. People who are living in houses they deem haunted report all manner of phenomena. You may not hear about Bigfoot and Nessie running around, but just about every other aspect of psychic–human-related–phenomena will be perceived or reported. Every unaccountable material phenomenon, too–every sound, shadow, or flicker of the lights–will seem to have a ghostly cause.

You can't prove any of it. You can't prove anybody saw a ghost. You can't prove anybody saw the Mother Mary at Lourdes, either. You can have multiple-witness sightings for Marian apparitions, but you have that for some house-ghosts. And you don't know for sure what they saw, and it would take a level of intuition I don't possess to tell you what it was. All you can prove is that they said they saw something. It's "exceptional human experience," EHE.

These old temples and churches are EHE-zones. Things built like them tend to be also, if very subtle ones. That could be why so many of our classic buildings in Buffalo are allegedly haunted: They are built with at least some of the specifics that the old-timers would have thought would encourage vision.

23

Map of the
Village of New Amsterdam
(now the City of Buffalo)
Made for the Holland Land Company
by
JOSEPH ELLICOTT, Surveyor.
1804.

VILLAGE
of
BUFFALO.

10 Chains to an Inch.

New York State

Lake Erie

Big Buffalo Creek

Little Buffalo Creek

1

The New Atlantis

Joseph Ellicott (1760-1826)
The 1804 Plan
Buffalo's Old Core and Niagara Square

Geomancy means, basically, "earth magic." In a working definition, geomancy is the idea that there are invisible forces in the earth that can be understood and plotted, and that they can affect the health, happiness, fortunes, and spirituality of individuals, societies, and entire regions. Preindustrial societies in all parts of the world have believed it, and their practices and philosophies have been maintained in unexpected ways–possibly in the design of Buffalo.

The occultists of Europe were said to have been very interested in the New World, particularly the young United States. To them, "the New Atlantis" seemed like a chance to start over, a chance to make a perfect new society and escape the problems of Europe, including a then-entrenched aristocracy and the perceived tyranny of a single religion. It was a chance to mold a world upon philosophy. It started with the capital city of the new union. Anyone exposed to the subject knows the depth of the symbolism and astronomy involved in the layout of Washington, DC. A few of the same people designed old Buffalo.

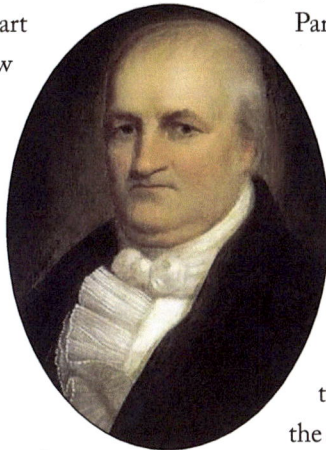

———

Born in 1760 on the day after Halloween, "the Father of Buffalo" Joseph Ellicott was of the third generation of his

Figure: 37

family to settle on this continent. His folk were Quakers. This bears a quick look–especially as the Quakers had a big footprint in Western New York, specifically settling the village of Orchard Park.

Most people think of the guy on the oatmeal box when they think of the Quakers. They did indeed start out as a starchy Protestant outfit who thought the British Anglicans were going soft–and that's saying something. Still, the Society of Friends has its mysteries. After all, their founder George Fox launched the faith after a vision he had atop Pendle Hill in Lancashire, England, in 1652. That's a funny place for a Christian epiphany, featuring megalithic monuments, Bronze Age burials, and centuries of rumors of being demon-haunted. Pendle Hill was thought to be the site of witch-celebrations (probably those of diehard pagans) and the focus of a sad saga just forty years before Fox's moment. In fact, a coven was suspected of holding its grim rites there, possibly as part of an arcane duel-to-the-death between rival witch-factions. (One was headed up by a woman whose witch/gang-name was "Demdike."

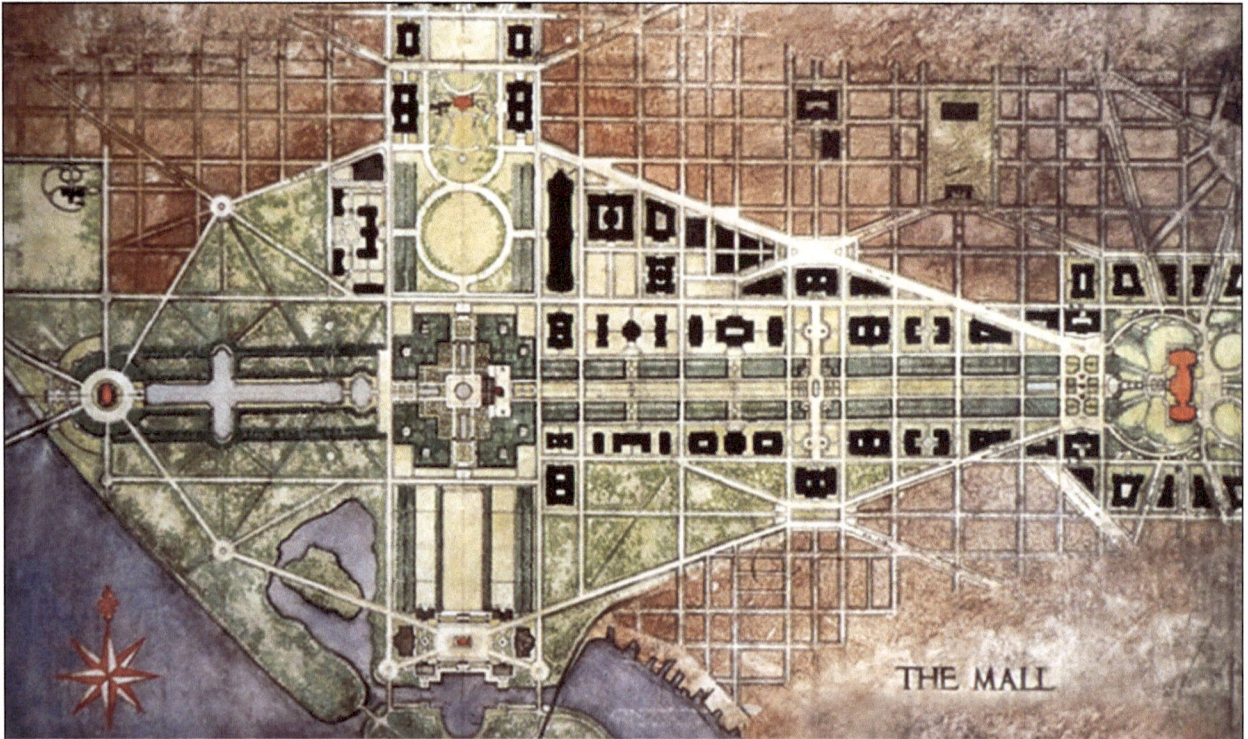

Figure: 39

The homies called the other "Chattox.") Ten of the crew were hung in 1612.

The Quakers tended to preserve old traditions, too, including that of "occult" architecture. They had a deep respect and sympathy for the First Nations of this continent. The Quakers were constantly involved in advising the Longhouse people on their rights. They were interested in exchanging with them, not exploiting or converting them. The Quakers were the one white outfit that the Six Nations/Longhouse folk never learned to distrust.

That second generation of Ellicotts who raised our Joseph were millers who set up a little Ponderosa in their part of Bucks County, PA. Joseph, Sr., was a Yankee tinkerer who built what sounds like his own combination clock, astronomical calculator, and music-box. It played twenty-four tunes. I wish we'd had better descriptions of it, because it had to be marvelous. I see where the Ellicott boys got their savvy.

In 1790 the federal government hired Andrew Ellicott to survey the new district where the capital city was to be built. Here's where things get interesting–for Buffalo.

Figure: 38

It's been said that, in the design of our nation's capitol, four great intellects stand out: Washington, L'Enfant, Jefferson, and Ellicott. By the last name is meant Andrew Ellicott, brother of Buffalo's founder.

Washington, DC was laid out according to late 18th-century mystical thought. Books are written on its geometry, symbolism, and alignments. Many of Washington's buildings and monuments, even recently-built ones, embody the type of occult architecture we'll soon talk about in Buffalo. Most obviously, the Washington Monument is modeled after Egyptian obelisks. Streets converging on the Capitol and Lincoln

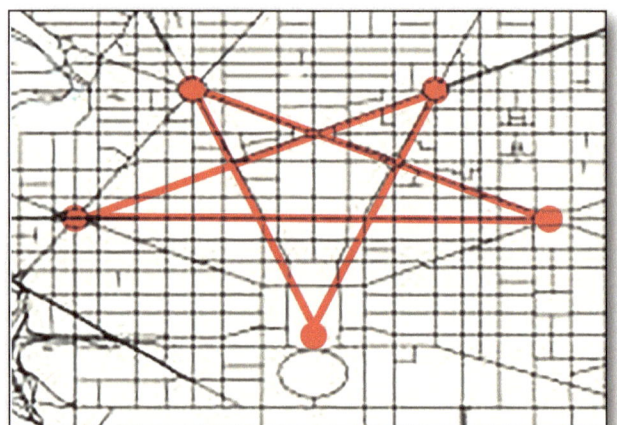

26

Park were arranged to form solstitial alignments. (From the Capitol lawn on the summer solstice, the sun rises in line with Maryland Avenue.) Compass points (as with the Great Pyramid) were also critical quotients in Washington's layout. This makes little sense to most of us now, but near the end of the 18th century this type of thought was not so offbeat. An undertaking as important as the capitol city of the new, "perfect" nation would be worth doing right from the roots up. Landscape layouts would be part of the deal.

The three conceptual architects of the young nation–George Washington, Ben Franklin, and Thomas Jefferson–were steeped in the philosophy of their day. The first two were Masons for sure, and all possibly Rosicrucians. (We've even heard speculation about them being Illuminists, AKA, Illuminati, which seems a stretch.)

The architect who gets public credit for Washington's design is the Frenchman, Major Pierre L'Enfant, an officer and engineer who had fought in the Revolutionary War. He had risen from Lieutenant to Major of Engineers and was 36 as he worked on Washington. L'Enfant may have known his Masonic symbolism, but George Washington canned his obstreperous ass halfway through. ("His obstinacy threw every difficulty in the way," wrote the Father of His Country.) Andrew Ellicott took over. He brought in brother Joseph as engineer and mathematician.

Andrew Ellicott was a multifaceted man: a distinguished engineer who had already served on state boundary commissions; an astronomer; the Geographer General of the United States; and vice-president of the American Philosophical Society in the chair often occupied by Franklin and Jefferson. Some of the speculations of that society would look pretty mystical to us now. They spun to at least some extent out of the continental "Natural Philosophers" who influenced the thought of the British Metaphysical poets, including Donne, Vaughan, and Marvell. Andrew was described as a spacey sort, a virtual artist and astronomer of the type that would be needed to lay out a mystical street plan. "Ellicott is always looking up to the stars," reported one of his Baltimore friends. "I am always looking to the ground. I

got some of the ground, but I don't think Ellicott got any of the stars."

Andrew Ellicott was on the Niagara in 1789 doing some scouting for the nation. The British snippily denied him permission to stay within the turf they reserved for themselves around Fort Niagara. Yes! Ten years after the end of the Revolution and the Brits were still claiming woofing rights over the Fort!

Brother Joseph was with him. He was well suited to cooking something up for Buffalo.

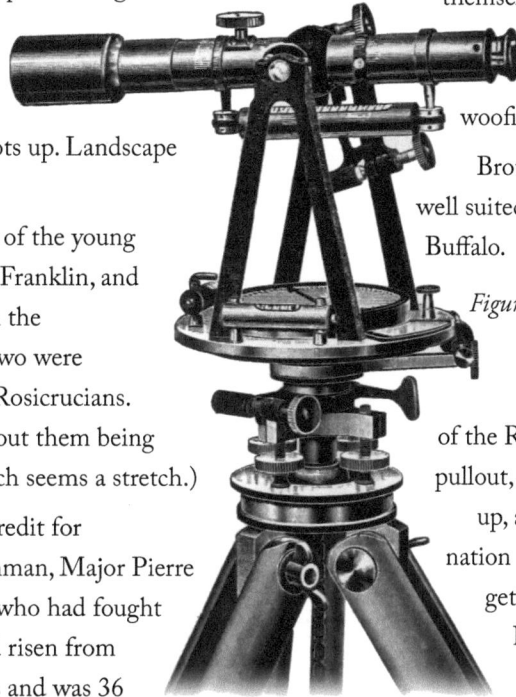

Figure: 40

———

Things were complicated at the end of the Revolution. As a result of the British pullout, a lot of undeveloped space opened up, and a young and basically coastal nation was starving to get at it. That meant getting the Grand Council of the Six Nations to sell much of their New York land to the United States.

White government's efforts to negotiate with the Six Nations Confederacy have never been helped by different cultural visions about land, possession, and treaties–and maybe even gender. It's notable that at many historic negotiations Longhouse women got up and said what they thought. I don't know of one in which the United States was represented by the voice of a single woman.

In 1794 George Washington's agent Timothy Pickering managed to get the deal done with the variably-named Treaty of Canandaigua. Thirteen Dutch investors bought three million acres, basically all of the state west of the Genesee River. The Holland Land Company formed to parcel it off for settlement, lot by lot. It hired Joseph Ellicott on the day he turned 40 to be its Resident Agent. That meant a lot of surveying and road-building. Ellicott had to be a mathematician, an astronomer, and a frontiersman. He was a big, burly man, well-suited by constitution for the job.

He started out building two major cart-paths on the Niagara Frontier. One was the Big Tree Road–today's

20A. It followed an ancient footpath that had connected Lake Erie and Seneca villages in the Finger Lakes for generations, possibly millennia. It's the main street of quite a few towns today between Hamburg and Geneseo, including Orchard Park, East Aurora, Wales, Varysburg, Warsaw, and Leicester. (FYI, you get a lot of ghost stories along 20A.)

The other was Transit Road, a north-south causeway that begins on a ridge in Orchard Park and shoots all the way to Olcott on Lake Ontario. Transit Road didn't follow any Native footpath. It was an artificial connector. Notice how laser-straight the road is even today from that high ground at its foot and the City of Lockport. Not for nothing was it given its name. The transit is a mounted mini-telescope, the tool of the day's surveyors. The one Joseph Ellicott used may have been the most advanced such device on the continent in his day.

———

When Joseph Ellicott took a look at the mouth of Buffalo Creek he saw an ideal lake harbor he was determined to make into a city. He planned on living in "New Amsterdam," too–the name surely being another tribute to his Dutch employers. His grand mansion would have been in today's downtown, on a long open patch by the Ellicott Square Building and the old Iroquois Hotel. His original plan even holds a dome-shaped arc on the east side of Main Street that confounded the city planners to come after him. ("Ellicott's Bow Window," they called it.)

The historians commend Ellicott's eye for the general location of his prospective new city. They don't say much about his choice for its precise core, Niagara Square. Neither does Ellicott himself, at least not that I can find. I would love to know what was there before all the landscaping. What about it called to him? I guess a visionary/sacred epiphany, had there been one, wouldn't be something you'd put into your annual reports to the suits. Maybe the type of planning we'd consider sacred in the Iron Age and occult in the digital age would have been fundamental in the 18th century. All I can divine is that this was a terrace, a high spot with a sublime overlook of the Erie, the Niagara, and Ontario, Canada, developing

even then. You'd be able to see it all today without the skyscrapers around it! I wouldn't be shocked if there had been some kind of earthwork at today's circle.

There was significance to the focal point with an earlier city plan Ellicott was involved with: Washington, DC. In *The Sacred Geometry of Washington DC*, Nicholas Mann describes Major L'Enfant's first step, finding a center from which everything else would radiate. With L'Enfant, we have no more information than that he picked an elevation for DC, the-then Jenkins' Hill. It is today's Capitol Hill. Maybe that was all it was.

Yet as Will Selman writes of L'Enfant, "As an art student in Paris and the son of an architect at Versailles, L'Enfant was versed in the ancient mathematical concepts of pi, the Fibonacci Sequence, and Phi or the Golden Mean, and the manner in which they were used in ancient Rome, Greece, and in the construction of the Egyptian Pyramids and the Temple of Solomon." Could there have been no other significance to Capitol Hill? To Buffalo's Niagara Square?

———

The town fathers came to have other ideas on Ellicott's bow window, as well as the city-name. They changed them both. Besides a gift for getting things done, Old Joseph seems to have had a knack for rubbing people wrong and getting ornery about it. In 1818 he left Buffalo to be "the Father of Batavia." ("Now let God take care of Buffalo," he was said to have remarked.)

He grew out of touch with Buffalo as the years went by, though he still considered the city his baby. He seems to have grown addled and was eventually fired for offending company clients. Word has it that old Joe started dressing in women's clothes, which wouldn't have played on the frontier. (On the 6'3" surveyor it would have been a look out of *Blazing Saddles*.) Probably not knowing how to interpret it in any other way, they sent him to Bellevue Hospital in New York City, where somehow he managed to hang himself in 1826.

Some say that Ellicott was a closeted Freemason and that his suicide came in connection with the Masonic scandal often called "the William Morgan Affair." That murder-conspiracy that tarred the entire American Lodge did indeed commence in Batavia, but linking Ellicott to it seems a hard sell for simple matters of timing. He was at Bellevue for two years before it broke.

―――――

Most of the world's cities never had a plan. They started out as villages where people gathered by water sources and trade routes. They built up from there, then hit a human center of gravity that was momentum in itself. When you

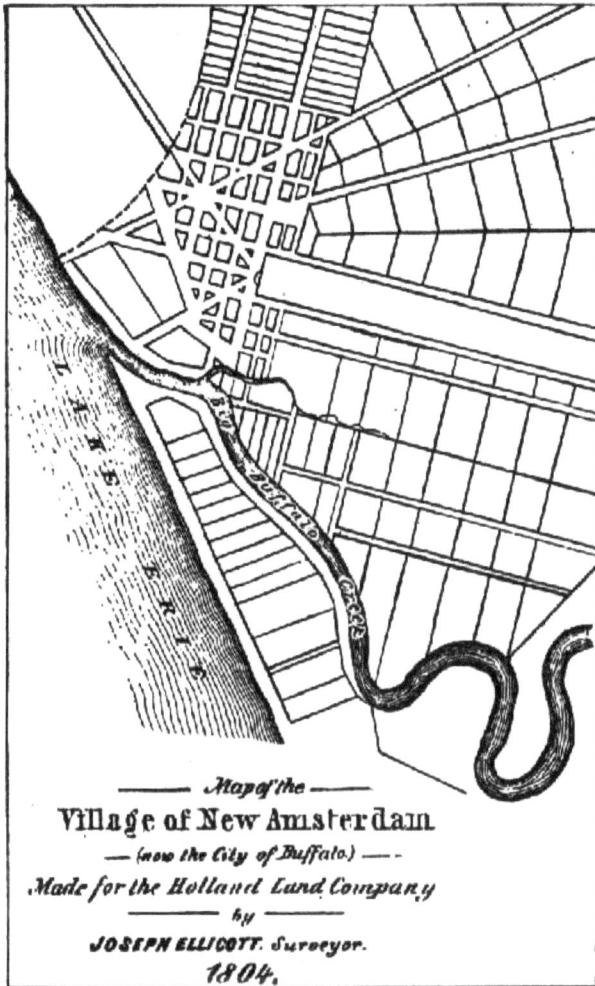

Figure: 41

get to one of these planned cities and there's an identifiable node–a heart-center–you have to at least check for a message. With Buffalo it's clearly Niagara Square.

The Ellicotts' 1804 street plan expresses the octagonal shape of the bagua, that fundamental feng shui chart. There's symbolism attached to the eight-sided form, some of which we'll get into later.

They say Joseph Ellicott's survey of Buffalo was based on astronomical observations and the establishment of the meridian. I'm not positive how much Andrew Ellicott helped with the design, but it's clear that Joseph's work in Washington influenced it. The "wheel" plan for Buffalo (radiating streets) was based on the work of engineers at Versailles and Philadelphia. Of course, it's a much smaller setup than would be needed even twenty years later. Most of the streets have new names today. (The original names seem tributes to rich Dutch investors and Joseph's Batavia bosses.) Even the street pointing laser-straight to Niagara Falls is named "Schimmelpennick Avenue" and not its present Niagara. Yet it runs right through Niagara Square, which was obviously the nucleus of the young town. I wonder what made Joseph Ellicott pick that precise spot.

Figure: 42a

Figure: 42b

Ancient First Nations trails and monuments have been incorporated into contemporary towns and cities elsewhere. Circleville, OH, was originally built around a large Hopewell-era henge (earth-circle). Randolph, NY, was at least partly built around a very big formation of the same apparent type, though I couldn't find a diagram for you. Maybe it was the same for Buffalo. I cannot assert something I cannot prove–but I can suspect it.

―――――

Hoping to learn what I could about Buffalo's original street plan, I contacted the late Steve Nelson, then living in Charlotte, NC, in 1996. Steve called himself "a mythic astrologer," which may sound a bit out there, but he was quite well educated on a range of esoteric subjects. I'd heard him speak in Ithaca in the early 1990s and been very impressed. A student of the sacred landscape and a well-known speaker and teacher, Steve had done intense research into the mysticism at the founding of our nation. I sent him Buffalo's layout and let him have a few weeks with it. When we spoke, I expected him to talk in nuts and bolts terms about sacred alignments and geometrical mysteries. As is so often the case when you interview a great mystic with a list of questions in mind, you seldom get what you were looking for. The answers you get can be worth so much more.

It's reasonable to suspect that Buffalo didn't just happen into the shape it is. According to Steve, there may have been a landscape-mythology in the occult/political circles in charge of setting the young nation up. Its figurative body was envisioned as having four cardinal points: Washington, Atlanta, Los Angeles–which existed since 1781 as a village–and Buffalo. The general logic of all that could have been based on many mystical systems, including astrology. It was thus important to get Buffalo with its northern bull-and-earth energies right from the beginning.

According to Nelson's sources, the nation's founders admired the Six Nations mystical traditions and believed

Figure: 43

in the power of the landscape. Ben Franklin encouraged the new citizens of the United States to shape their towns and villages along Native patterns, which often followed natural energy lines in the earth. [When I pointed out to Steve that the central roadways of Buffalo and its region (Routes 5, 20, and 16) were all once ancient trails, he chuckled as if he should have guessed.] There was a considerable Native mystical legacy in the region when Buffalo was forming.

Buffalo was settled decades before it was christened, yet its official birthday, the day of its incorporation (April 20, 1832), makes Buffalo, astrologically speaking, a first-degree Taurus city, with a grand trine (Sun, Moon, and Saturn) in earth. This is interesting, since the buffalo, the American animal for which the city is apparently named, corresponds to the European bull-symbol Taurus.

Buffalo's chart told Steve that there are lots of resources in Buffalo, both spiritual and material. Its energies involve earth and water, the terrestrial two of the Greek four elements. In that sense, it's a good place to get grounded. This is right in keeping with Buffalo's image as a blue-collar town: Its citizenry will work hard and pay their taxes, but few will set Hollywood on fire.

Nelson turned Buffalo's plan over to Darley Adare, a map-dowser, a long-range finder of energy. She felt sure that Niagara Square was the heart-center of the city and identified three major lines of force all radiating to or from it. The big one comes down Niagara Street, pointing right to that natural power-point Niagara Falls. Another originates at Gates Circle and wends down Delaware Avenue. (Don't forget that Delaware runs ley-straight between the Square and Gates Circle, once an impressive natural fountain.) The third energy-line is Genesee Street, which as Buffalo's mystical artist and "urban shaman" Franklin LaVoie observes heads right to an earth-mound he can spy in the distance but has never identified. Is it human-made? Is it an ancient Hopewellian-style monument?

Steve Nelson called these energy-lines the spiritual lifelines of the city, beacons of power that lure all kinds of tappers, natural and supernatural. He pointed out that most of the hauntings in his native Charlotte are along these force-lines, some of which may be leys. Steve's feeling was that somebody, possibly Joseph Ellicott, used dowsing to settle the location of Niagara Square.

Though the Square is not precisely an octagon, the streets that once shot from it in eight directions evoke that symbol to the same effect. Its location and composition–its obelisk, fountain, and siting–make it, in geomantic terms, a rare accumulator of telluric power. The Square brings energies in from all the lines. It's a "resonator" for the entire region. The Egyptianate McKinley Monument stands at the center. "Obelisks are like tuning forks when they're at the center of a convergence of streets," reported Steve. "The vibes go in all directions."

Based on its official birthday–July 26, 1788–New York

is a Leo state. Steve sensed that Buffalo is an earthy spot of it in need of an energizing influence, like fire. He suggested that a big garnet (the state stone, a fire-symbol) be placed at Niagara Square, giving the region a better balance of Leo energy. A perpetual flame might help here, too, where an ounce of prevention would be tons of cure. It's perhaps in keeping with Steve's recipe for Buffalo that lions–symbols of primal fire–were placed about the McKinley Monument. (Even they seem to need a zap, though; they're lounging leos.)

Steve Nelson was quick to mention to me, though, that those lines of force–Niagara, Delaware, and Genesee–need to flow. The ch'i of the city needs to 'breathe' through them. "You guys need to be real careful up there," he said, "not to block any of those off, at least not real close to the city-core." He was working off the 1804 map. I should have sent him a more recent one. Too late.

The work for City Hall in 1929 was the first disruption of the Force, cutting off Court Street from the west. That was the start of the Great Depression. Now we have the Buffalo Niagara Convention Center (1978), cutting off the Genesee a few blocks northeast of Niagara Square. Whatever impact it might have could explain some of the region's most public flops, including the fickle fate of our major sports teams. Wide right. No goal. "Home run throwback." (I mean, "forward pass.") The refereeing that whole game with the Eagles in November 2023. Sheeesh.

———

Washington, DC, is aligned on the cardinal directions. Buffalo's axis is a nudge–15°–east of due North. That's about 12:20 (little hand) on a clockface. That had to be deliberate. Ellicott knew how to establish his points. What could it mean?

Franklin Lavoie suggested to me once that there could be some connection between Buffalo's original plan and Teotihuacan, an enigmatic Mexican city that was the home base of a lost empire. Teotihuacan is a good example of the Mesoamerican tradition of planning cities, settlements, and buildings as reflections of the Universe. Teotihuacan's urban grid was laid out upon a single axis, 15.5° east of north. This little slant could not have been accidental, either. There were expert astronomers and

builders in Teotihuacan. That alignment is half a degree from that of Buffalo. Take a look on the map at Delaware Avenue emanating out of Niagara Square and tell me what you think. It could be close enough to be a tribute to the Teo axis.

Why would anyone echo an ancient American city-layout? There I think I have you. It's an old pattern among the Western occult groups, particularly the Freemasons, to pay tribute to earlier traditions. The Masons of the New World were very interested in the mysticism of the First Nations, particularly the Iroquoian Six Nations and the urbanized cultures of Mesoamerica. Their reasons weren't entirely DEI. To many of the early American Masons, Masonry was a global faith, and they hoped to prove it so, possibly because it "grounds" their disciplines in older ones.

Buffalo's northeastern wobble has another overtone. The Freemasons are fond of making statements involving that direction. Many Masonic cornerstones are set to the northeast, for instance. This could be because in the northern climes the sun on the summer solstice rises in the northeast–and St. John's Day/MidSummer's Day is one of the two big commemorations in Masonry.

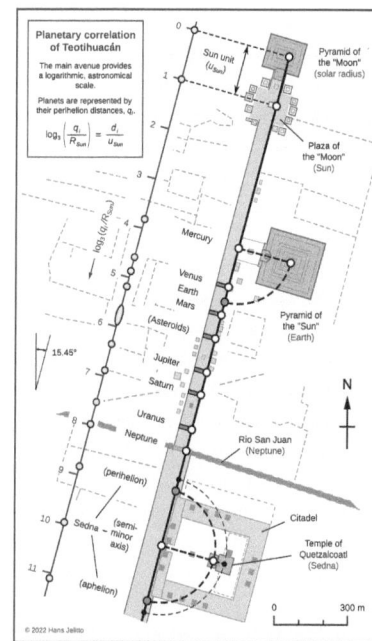

Was Ellicott a Freemason? Some clues are there, though his biographers don't seem convinced of it. It would have been unusual in a prominent frontiersman not to have some exposure to the Craft.

There's a mystery, though, with that Teo-connection. What could Joseph Ellicott have known about an ancient Meso-city? About an extinct civilization? What could anyone have known in 1804?

Figure: 44

31

At least some understanding would have been possible. The Aztecs knew about Teotihuacan, having found it abandoned in the Middle Ages. So did the Spaniards. Excavations that would have been cursory by today's standards were carried out as early as the late 1600s. Maybe those would have uncovered that curious alignment. Maybe the 15°-connection has a broader significance that has escaped me. The Freemasons, for instance, make a big deal sometimes about latitudinal and longitudinal coordinates.

Sometimes the geometry, the numerology, and other specifics have cross-cultural significance on their own. Imagine the old city plan in a circle. That 15° cutout leaves 345° which could be intended to suggest the 3-4-5 Pythagorean right triangle, usually thought of as the Egyptian triangle.

———

Figure: 45

There's another geomantic gesture out of Niagara Square, and it's not one of Steve Nelson's power-lanes. It's Court Street. It's one of the most dramatic configurations in any contemporary city, and it's a true ley–a straight-line connector of sacred/monumental sites. The best place to observe it at land-level would probably be from the Soldiers and Sailors Memorial at Lafayette Square, unveiled in 1882. From there you can look right up Court Street to the McKinley obelisk (1907) and dead-center City Hall (1931).

It's an awesome sight, and you may notice the two Meso-style towers of the Liberty Building (1925) on your left perfectly paralleling the line of your gaze. Maybe they were intended to be conscripted into the ley. Maybe they just follow the street. Surely the last piece to fall in place, City Hall, was wittingly sited. The ley goes up the heart of its tower.

Court Street's east-southeast alignment looks perpendicular to Delaware Avenue, which means it could

be perpendicular to the Teo-axis. Obviously this could all have evolved from Joseph Ellicott's original plan without meaning to make a message.

What isn't a mystery is the fact that making a statement with a perpendicular across distance is not unparalleled in North America. Remember the astonishing "Hopewell Highway," the 2000 year-old dead-straight trackway across the state of Ohio between two nearly identical octagon-and-circle earthworks at Newark and Chillicothe oriented to be perpendicular to each other. That sixty-mile road may once have been paved and walled.

———

The remarkable artist and polymath Daniel Smith of East Aurora and Charleston, SC, has spent time trying to figure out the esoteric significance of Western New York. I reached out to him for insights on the archaeoastronomy of Buffalo, and he was well prepared to respond.

Probably calibrated right out of Niagara Square, Buffalo's latitude is officially 42.880230 N. Working with it as 43° and envisioning a compass set like a clock face dead-center atop Niagara Square, Daniel informs us that on the day of the winter solstice, the sun should rise from the southeast at 123.° That means it should set across it at 303.° I marked that as a blue beam on this diagram, and I don't spot any relevant connections in Ellicott's original plan or in the city as it is today. With the summer solstice we may have a match. The sun on that day ought to rise at around 57° and set at around 237.° On my diagram, the Midsummer sunrise line is fairly close to overlapping Genesee Street coming into Niagara Square. That tags on another front. Genesee is one of Steve Nelson's powerlines. And Midsummer, let us remember, is the Masonic power-day.

My calculations have to be considered inexact. I'm no astronomer or surveyor, and any blunder in my own plotting would throw things off. But it seems as likely as not that Genesee Street gestures to the line of the summer solstice sunrise. Every Midsummer's day we might have been able to camp at the Square and had our own sacred Manhattanhenge–that moment when a sunrise or -set flows up a major city street–that is, if we hadn't messed so much with the sight-lines here in

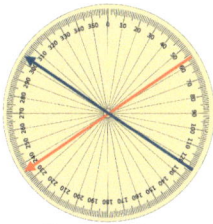

Figure: 46

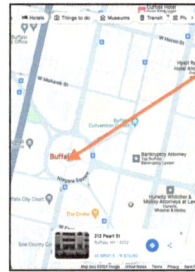

Figure: 47

Buffalo. That Genesee was a bad street to cut off from a number of perspectives.

———

If there's a core of energy at Niagara Square that might manifest itself into a wake of hauntings, the signs are there. It would be hard to find a grand building bordering that bagua without ghost- or wonder-stories to be found. I used to lead a whole tour based simply on the Square. That's what you'd expect for a site of geomantic power–"earth energy." It gets people saying they see things. It's an EHE-zone. It can put them into moods.

In my college years I had a holiday-season job downtown. At the lunch hour I often walked to Niagara Square. The days were mild, moist, grey, and still, far from the white tempests typecast of the Niagara winter. I remember being haunted by some mood that came over me at Niagara Square as if a meditative influence beckoned from it and grew as I neared. I felt the yearning to lounge there, to write in my journal, or just reflect. Lines of poetry came to the mental ear. It was as if I sensed something as a college kid that I know now I ought to have.

At Stonehenge I would have been on the lookout for epiphanies. American cities seemed to me then the opposite of reflection-givers. I give my younger self a lot of credit for that–sensing the energy. Our Six Nations friends would call it *orenda*.

———

This article is less a boast of authority than a call to attention, even a cry for help. Mysteries are hidden in the foundations of some of our cities, and we may have been left with one at the heart of Buffalo. The verification either way would call for the contributions of specialists in a variety of disciplines, both practical and arcane. Yet one of the signs of an energy about a space would be that it impacts people who don't know it ought to be there. We thank Nancy J. Parisi's wry *Buffalo Spree* article for reminding us that we don't have to wait for the New Age to see it at Niagara Square.

Someone sold Mayor Stanley Makowski's administration on the idea that the classical fountain and Egyptianate monument at the city's heart could use beautification of a modernist variety. Those "improvements" turned the Square into a brickwork bagel only muggers and revolutionaries would have appreciated. If the Revolution had come in 1976, it would have been the site of someone's last stand. Behind its ponderous terra-cotta crenels the square's graceful lions barely peeped. Its classical fountain cowered like a koi pond, and its pale obelisk shot startlingly skyward like a missile ready to launch above sandbags. It brought the public to a curious outrage. The only people who dealt with it much were the circling motorists one would think too busy to notice, yet it may affirm the spiritual significance of the site that simply obstructing the view of it touched such a nerve.

Too long into the rising rhetoric, the Mayor backed his planners. At the expense of several hundred thousand taxpayer dollars, "Fort Makowski" was disassembled, and in many minds the phrase came to stand for a good man's embattled term as mayor.

Figure: 48

2
The Way of Wind and Water

Frederick Law Olmsted (1822-1903)
Delaware Park
84 Parkside Avenue, Buffalo

In Things That Go Bump in the Night *(1959), New York folklorist Louis C. Jones put forts and churches at the top of his list of American structures that collect ghost stories. Hotels and schools came in soon after. Hospitals aren't far back on my list. Most North Americans do indeed expect their ghosts to stay indoors, and think it strange to hear them reported in broad, open, fairly natural spaces. Yet, as Hamlet says, "as a stranger, give it welcome." When we think of all the haunted hills, valleys, lanes, and groves in world-tradition–and burial grounds and battlefields!–it shouldn't seem so queer that a big stretch of greenspace like Delaware Park and its bookend Forest Lawn Cemetery might collect ghostly folklore. Welcome, too, the man who made the Park, "the father of American landscape architecture." Frederick Law Olmsted touched so many places in Buffalo that the attempt even to sketch him is daunting.*

I remember a story about a celebrated American musician whom I think was trumpeter Wynton Marsalis. As a student at one of our academies, Marsalis wrote a solo for his instructors and brought it proudly to class. It was intricate and technically perfect, and few student musicians in the world could have played it. His teacher took a quick look, crumpled it up, and threw it in the waste basket.

"Why did you do that?" said our young friend.

"Because it's packed with notes," was the reply. "There's nowhere in it for the song to breathe."

Marsalis thought about that and realized that his teacher had been right. Those occasional pauses in an improvisational piece can be as important as any note the listener hears. Architects, too, get inspiration from music, and with the work of the best, what the observer is meant to imagine can be as significant as what is there to be seen.

———

When the Europeans touched down on the American continents, the Six Nations/Longhouse People of upstate New York didn't have a true Devil. Their system included a number of divinities, including two important ones who worked differently, but not in a state of conflict. The first whites were, perhaps naturally, expecting a God-Devil opposition, and they translated the names of these two grand beings as "The Good-Minded Spirit" and "The Bad-Minded Spirit." There they've generally rested for centuries. Ah, it seems the plight of the Western mind to like things in polarities: all good or all bad; light vs. dark. My Native contacts suggest that the translations for

Opposite Page - Figure: 49

35

these two figures might better have been, "Clear-Minded Spirit" and "Tangle-Minded Spirit." It goes back to their Creation-tale:

A giant water bird dove after prey into the primal sea. The mud it brought up became the land. The primal female, the earth-mother, gave birth to twin sons. One of these great earth-born spirits was the embodiment of a principle of earthly features—gentle, nurturing, pastoral places ideal for human living—with related qualities, substances, and beings. The other stood for the landscape-challenges: sharp vertical forms, crags, declivities, and a range of other associations.

It wasn't that the Tangled One was evil. He was just offbeat. The direct path didn't work for him. More Trickster than demon—more Loki than Satan—he liked intricate operations and the indirect way of getting places. He liked shadows and twilights, not noon. He liked winding wooded trails and not open lanes.

There are hints of a landscape-mysticism among the Longhouse people, the Six Nations, of the upstate. So far the ethnologists have not developed it. It does not surprise me that major components of Six Nations spirituality could exist and yet escape academic notice. Their traditions have never been fully given to the rest of the world. I know this because in my talks and interviews with the Elders and storytellers I've known among the Seneca, Tuscarora, and other Northeastern nations I detect things I've never seen in the written record. Those philosophies and attitudes to the forces of the earth may be based on these antinomies, the open and the tangled, the soothing and the sharp.

The Asians have something like that, too, and it's not hidden. It's called *feng shui*. Its variables are yin and yang.

———

New York's place names can be mighty interesting. Some are queer, puckish, and fodder for trivia. Some go back to whatever the First Nations folk called some feature in the region. The not-always precise translations we are left with today suggest the impressions the first whites got from them.

Some of New York's place-names are sinister.

Ellicottville has Witch Hollow Road. We have

Figure: 50

Witches' Walk and Witch-Light Hill near Salamanca. There's a Witches' Hole State Forest not far west of New Paltz.

There are several Spook Lanes or Spook Hills, one in Yates County and one, I believe, in Cattaraugus. Cayuga County boasts a Spook Woods.

Queens holds a Snake Road and Bridgehampton a Snake Hollow. We have a couple of Snake Hills, one near Newburgh and another on the east side of Saratoga Lake. The latter is an enduring mystery to me, all the more because people seem to want to keep something about it quiet. They say there's an old monument atop it, possibly a burial mound that long preceded the arrival of the whites.

We have, by my count, fifteen "Devil-somethings" in just the dozen or so counties generally considered to

Figure: 51

comprise Western New York. We have a Devil's Hole in Lewiston, Colden, and Clarence. We have the Devil's Rock in Stafford. We have the Devil's Bathtub and the Devil's Punchbowl in Rochester. We have a trail called "the Devil's Backbone" in Cattaraugus County and the

Devil's Pool in Chautauqua.

Some of these are indeed sublime places, even hazardous. Just to look at them fires the imagination. Others–groves, vales, and lanes–look peaceful and even nurturing. You have trouble figuring out what the excitement would be about.

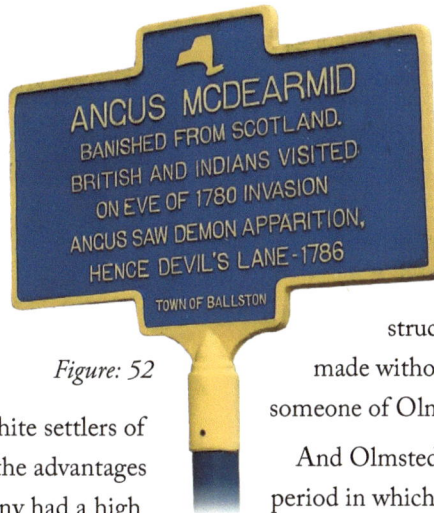

Figure: 52

Yet remember, most of the first white settlers of the Northeast were not gifted with the advantages of cross-cultural enlightenment. Many had a high mistrust of non-Christian cultures. We'd consider their attitudes to be basically fundamentalist. If something was not Godly, it seemed diabolical by default.

As the Six Nations elder pointed to a hill and said, *orenda*–their word for the power of earth, life, and spirit– the white trader heard only "magic." If an Algonquin -speaker gestured to a valley and said the equivalent, *manitou*, the frontier minister heard only "witch." What they would have been saying in either case was that the area indicated had some kind of natural-supernatural power that the First Nations folk had sensed and respected for centuries. Some of our place-names can be keys to this.

———

At the April 1998 conference of the New England Antiquities Research Association, New York filmmaker Ted Timreck delivered a unique power-point presentation on Frederick Law Olmsted and his landscape-designs. Its title based on Northeastern place-names, "The Devil's Footstep" noted that Olmsted's balanced use of natural features is bizarrely coincident with the way of regarding them in Iroquois and Algonquin creation myths. This is like the Asian ideas of yin and yang, and their enactment into landscape like feng shui. This way of regarding natural features is non-Western. Those who need it explicated should turn to Timreck, whose insight this is.

It was Timreck's implication that "the father of American landscape architecture" could have been exposed to both these Eastern and North American Indian mystical systems, and that they could have been

manifested in his designs. Olmsted left at an impressionable age–21–for a year in China, where the mysticism of the landscape would have been no secret. Every village had someone trained in feng shui, and few decisions about anything to do with structures or their siting would have been made without a consultation. It would be hard for someone of Olmsted's persuasions to have avoided it.

And Olmsted spent plenty of time in the upstate at a period in which the Six Nations folk might have been talking a little freer, especially with someone in whom they felt respect and sympathy. If Olmsted had a faintly curious mind about such subjects, he'd have had little trouble establishing a communication, most likely with the Oneida or Onondaga of the eastern Finger Lakes and possibly the few Mohawk left in the Hudson Valley. He seems to have had his philosophies set by the time he got to Buffalo.

———

The Europeans had some clue about the power of landscape, too, though by historic times maybe only the artists could sense it.

Romanticism was an artistic protest movement that swept across Europe in the late 1700s and a few decades into the 19th century. To simplify it, Romanticism was a rebellion against earlier styles of art–like neoclassicism– plus the systematization of the Industrial Revolution, the conformity of thought associated with mainstream religion, and everything associated with urbanization. A major theme in Romanticism is a basic pantheist, even animist, revival. Nature–capital N–was a god in itself, and every blade of grass had a spirit that represented a nerve in the body of the world.

"The Romantic Landscape" is a way to describe the sort of human-touched natural space that seems inspiring to many minds. There are usually said to be two styles of it:

The Pastoral: a tender, human-friendly, environment said to express "man's dominion" over the natural world. There's often a touch here and there of architectural features, typically classical, like Greek columns and

temples. In painting it often includes farm scenes, either contemporary or antique.

The Sublime: untouched, wild, and even dangerous nature. One feature of Romantic art, literature, and painting was to show the grandeur and mystery in Nature and emphasize the smallness of human beings and the limitations of human power. The British landscapist J. M. W. Turner (1775-1851) once had himself lashed to the bow of a ship during a storm so he could experience the full power of Nature–then paint it.

————

Frederick Law Olmsted was born in Hartford, CT, into a family of successful merchants with two centuries of roots on this continent–and a love of nature and inquiry. Young Fred was starting up at Yale, but on one of his nature-rambles he did a face-plant into a patch of the Eastern weed poison sumac. For months he could hardly see, and the college plan was off the table. After stints as a seaman and a merchant, Olmsted settled into life on a

farm on Staten Island and a thriving career as a journalist. Sent to tour and write about the American South, he became a devout Abolitionist. He thought slavery was the root of all the South's problems, oppressing blacks and whites alike and squeezing out a true middle class.

A trip to England in 1850 made another big impact on him. The British Isles are not the easiest places to grow anything. ("We have two seasons," some of the residents say, "July and autumn.") Maybe because of their impermanence, the English seem to have loved their gardens as long as they've been the English. Maybe inspired by the villas of the Roman occupation, they developed grand, monumental, Renaissance -style gardens, with tasteful mixes of crafted features like arches, trellises, and pathways onto groomed landscapes.

Surely some of the shapes and symbols of Renaissance mysticism– like alchemy and Rosicrucianism– could have appeared, too, in these delicate features we style with the name, "the English garden." Pacing those pathways could have been treading the form of a magical symbol.

Figure: 54

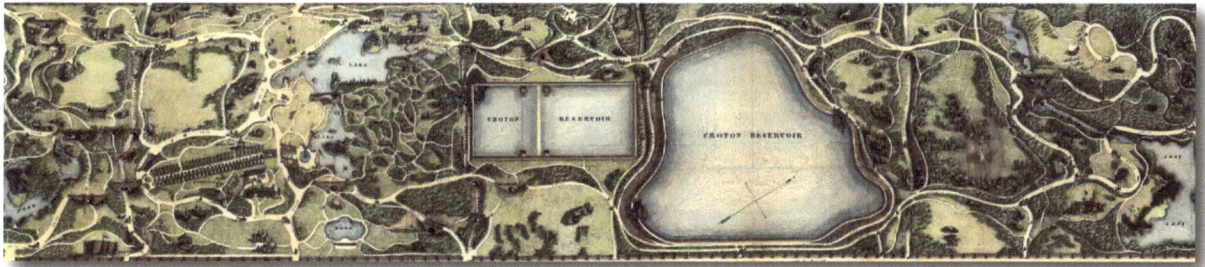

Figure: 57

It did not surprise Olmsted to find that these gardens were the domains of the rich and noble, not the public. He was predisposed to see little good in the thought, culture, or design he associated with the elites of Europe and the American South. Yet his reaction to one of the

Figure: 56

few public English gardens, Joseph Paxton's Birkenhead Park near Liverpool, was admiration for "the manner in which art had been employed to obtain from nature so much beauty… I was ready to admit that in democratic America there was nothing to be thought of as comparable with this People's Garden." A passion was launched in him, to bring natural beauty to all classes in the land of his birth–and particularly into the urban areas where population was high and green space already running short.

His mission was a worthy one. It may shock us now, but even in Olmsted's day the Industrial Revolution was running roughshod over natural landscapes. People were rapidly moving to the cities and enduring the problems of overcrowding. Olmsted blamed urban tensions on this loss of touch with woods, hills, and open air. Like many Romantics and Transcendentalists, Olmsted saw that connection as a vital one to the human spirit. He had no immediate way to put his calling into action.

A friendship with the New York landscape architect Andrew Jackson Downing was another turning point. Through Downing, editor of *The Horticulturalist* magazine, Olmsted met the English-born architect Calvert Vaux (1824-1895). (Vaux "rhymes with talks," according to Buffalo's Francis Kowsky, and "fox" according to author Hugh Howard.) Vaux and Downing had planned to enter the contest to design the proposed New York Central Park, but Downing was killed in July, 1852, in the notorious explosion on the Hudson River steamboat *Henry Clay*. Olmsted had never planned a landscape, but Vaux took him on as a partner. The pair won–a career-launching move. They went on to a program of grand parks and landscape designs that marks many American cities today.

In 1859, Olmsted married his brother's widow, Mary Cleveland (Perkins), and adopted her three children–his nephews and niece. Two children of theirs survived infancy, daughter Marion and son Frederick, Jr.

Balding at an early age, Olmsted was unimposing in size or manner. He had, though, the gift of many social and political connections, especially through The Century Club, a New York men's association. The United States' most prominent poet, William Cullen Bryant, and Hudson River School painter F. E. Church were

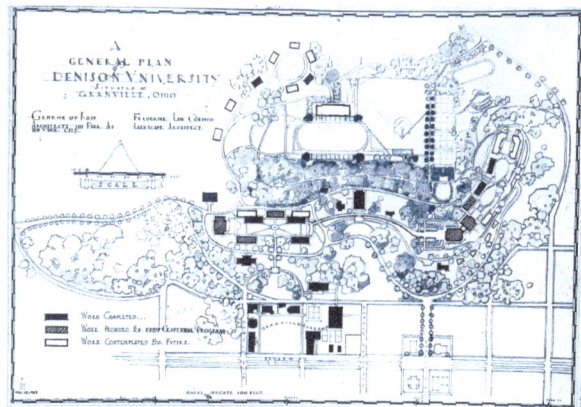

Figure: 58

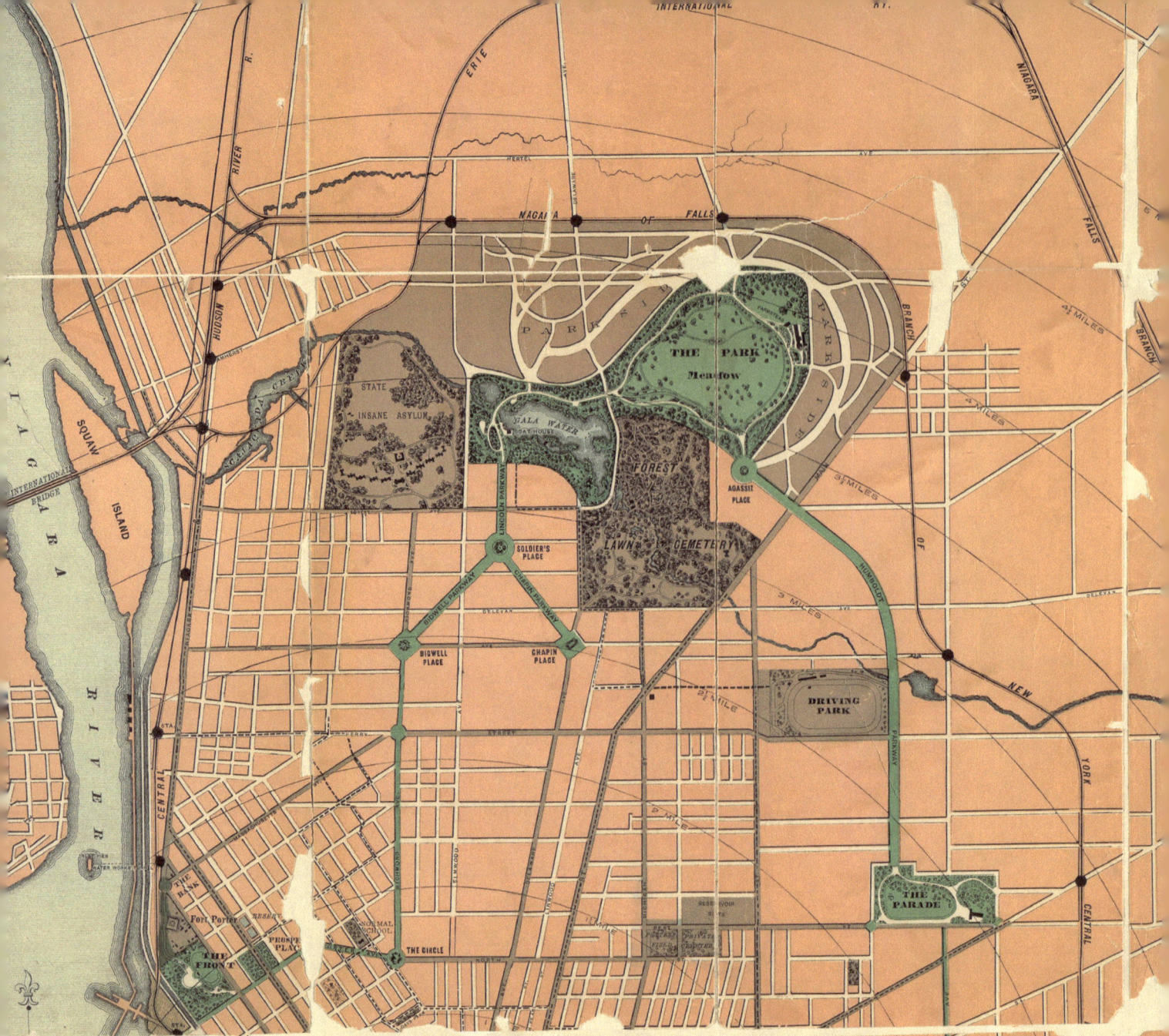

OLMSTED'S
Sketch Map
OF
BUFFALO

Showing the relation of the

Park System

Centurions–and personal friends. So was another important friend-to-be, the architect H. H. Richardson.

Success fell on Olmsted's work like a golden rain. "He paints with lakes and wooded slopes," said architect Daniel Burnham, "with lawns and banks and forest-covered hills; with mountainsides and ocean views."

Olmsted was not a flamboyant man, which made him such a contrast to, perhaps, his most impactful friend, the portly and ribald Richardson. When the pair strolled landscapes or jested at parties they must have looked like the old comedy team Laurel and Hardy–or Hal and Falstaff. Yet this friendship was an aesthetic partnership that would last twenty years. They shared a vital simpatico. With the grandest of projects, they felt, the man-made structure was half the impact. The siting was the rest. That perhaps explains our Buffalo Psychiatric Center, whose grounds so crucial, everyone thought, to healing were sculpted by Olmsted and Vaux, whose informal partnership came largely to an end in 1873.

Figure: 60

By 1895, Olmsted could feel himself wobbling, and he retired from public and professional life. His son and his adopted nephew John Charles continued the work. Under the name of The Olmsted Brothers, they took on a number of projects including college campuses like that of my alma mater, Denison University in Granville, OH.

While the hand of the father of American landscape architecture may not have touched Denison's design, its influence may be felt. Typical of a Renaissance plan, Denison's West Quad is laid out to have gorgeous meditative spaces. I almost never saw students exploiting them for reflection when I was there. (DU did have the

Opposite Page - Figure: 59

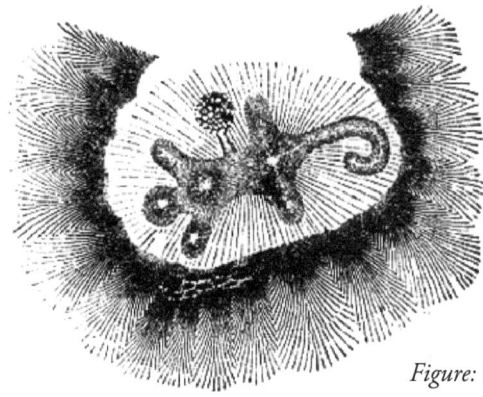

Figure: 61

rep of a party school.) Yet there are mysteries. An ancient earthwork was said to rest upon the hilltop that forms the campus' base. Six miles as it is from the monument complex at Newark, it was probably produced by the Hopewell culture. Curiously, too, on a hill about a mile from the one that supports dear Denison is a still-extant earthwork often called "the Alligator Mound." (It probably represents "the Water-Panther," an earth-and-water being working counterpoint to the pan-Northeastern sky-being, the Thunderbird.) In sight of Denison's Swasey Chapel as it is, the Alligator Mound might have made some astronomical statement with either the monument on the DU campus or even one of the features at Newark.

By 1898 Olmsted moved to Belmont, MA, and spent his last five years as a patient at the McLean Hospital. He had submitted a design for its grounds that had never been executed. What were his thoughts, gazing out the windows and imagining what could have been made of it? All left of him lies today in Hartford, CT, in the Old North Cemetery.

———

Olmsted's Parkway system in Buffalo was not only his biggest project but the first system of parkways to be developed for any American city. He was involved in so much Buffalo-area work that a thoughtful treatment of it all–even without supernatural folklore–would be the work of a book.

By my count in the city alone, Olmsted and Vaux designed: four significant parks, all still with us, though much-modified; seven glorious parkways, four of which we still have; seven places and circles, six of which we keep in some form; and five smaller city parks, one of which we maintain.

South of the city core, the energetic pair laid out three parks, two parkways, and two circles, all of which we have, more or less. North of the city, Olmsted laid out or contributed designs for one park and two parkways, one that was never built and one, Humboldt Parkway, scourged by "urban renewal" and the notorious Scajaquada Expressway, Robert Moses' rooting, tooting racecourse through Delaware Park. (Your state and city planners at work.)

————

Olmsted was heavily influenced by the poetic and philosophical forces of Romanticism and its American stepchild-with-a-mind-of-its-own, Transcendentalism. For Olmsted, each landscape had its own unique integrity. His job was to evoke its *genius loci*, its spirit of place, with as little manipulation as possible. Nature could not be improved upon; it could merely be revealed. It reminds me of Michelangelo seeing the angel inside the marble block. ("I carved until I set him free.") It reminds me, too, of the barely-worked stones of the megalithic monuments of Europe. The point there seemed to be to let each stone stay as close as possible to what it was before having been moved to make the human pattern.

For Olmsted, the message of a design was aimed at the inner self, the unconscious mind. It was subliminal, and so much of the time he, like several of our architects, was the only one who could fully see it. His goal was a design that did not mark itself, yet all would take it in and be eased. Just look at his triumph in Saratoga Springs, NY, the haunting, enveloping Congress Park. It's tiny, but you forget that you are in a city when you set your first step into that bowl of tranquility and approach the spring, pool, and classical stonework.

————

As the human body has its meridians that can be soothed with massage or acupuncture, so the earth may have its own lines of force–and its nodes where those force-lines cross. Maybe these nodes are what the dowsers find. Maybe they cause a lot of your hauntings. Maybe this is what Olmsted could react to. Maybe other societies had it figured out a long time ago.

Nicknamed "Chinese geomancy," feng shui is pronounced, *fung shway*. The words mean, "the Way of Wind and Water." It is the Asian system for interpreting the message of landscape. The masters use the bagua, that ornamental, octagonal chart, to interpret the energies of place.

Feng shui can detect visual patterns productive of human and animal content and prosperity. It can detect earthly and material patterns of helpful or harmful energies.

Buffalo-based Certified Feng Shui Practitioner and teacher Linda Ellson points out that feng shui operates on the principles of yin and yang.

The yang force is open, bold, and solar. The yang landscape is a broad hill that seems to step forth to be observed. It's a spacious lawn that spreads itself before the sun. It's uplifting.

The yin force can be moody, declivitous, and dark. The yin landscape could be a shady nook, even a dim grove or a precipitous valley. It has intrigue, perhaps even danger. It's sublime, if not a little forbidding. Edmund Burke and his mid-18th century contemporaries regarded this quality with phrases like "terrible delight" and "savage beauty."

Except as a teaching-tool, seeing yin and yang as opposites is probably improper. They are too entwined for that. Like the clear and the tangled, neither one is truly sinister, either. The only thing that matters is balance. Part of Olmsted's genius might have been his gift for evoking the potential of a space to reflect the balance that would be right for it–and that would be most intriguing, healing, and even visionary for its human beholders.

Linda Ellson interprets the essence of balance in Olmsted's work through the lens of feng shui. In her words, "The natural elements present in his landscape designs symbolize the five Asian elemental forces. Trees and flowers embody the Wood element. Ponds and fountains represent Water. Lamp posts evoke Fire. Meandering stone pathways symbolize Earth, and sturdy steel and iron benches epitomize Metal. In this intricate dance of elements, Olmsted brought forth the inherent harmony of a space."

————

Few Buffalonians today have a sense of how open and

wild the region along the Scajaquada Creek was for the city's first half-century. One August afternoon in 1868 Olmsted took a carriage ride out just north of Forest Lawn Cemetery with his Buffalo friend William Dorsheimer (1832-1888), the Congressman, New York Lieutenant Governor, and "man of culture" (a la Francis Kowsky). They came to a landscape of deep old-growth woods and cleared meadows, of which Dorsheimer remarked that a little expense could give the place "a park-like character."

"Here is your park," said Olmsted in a scan. "Almost ready-made."

When people in Buffalo used to say, "The Park," everybody knew they meant the northern hub of Olmsted's Buffalo system. At 350 square acres, Delaware Park is one of the relatively few "true" parks that Olmsted by his own definition created.

By a park, Olmsted meant an urban oasis, a grand space in which the visitor could lose all sense of being in a city. By a "true" park, Olmsted meant one with three distinct environments: a big water body like the present Hoyt Lake; a big meadow; and groves of wood. Indeed, this mix of "wildness and disorder," wrote a Chicago reporter, was an Olmsted signature. Every feature of his greatest finished works displayed "but a careful oversight of nature's own simple ways."

Completed in 1870, Delaware Park has to be considered a companion to another green space, Forest Lawn Cemetery. The sense of division we feel between the twain today is due to 20th century engineering. Bearing their picnic baskets and wheeling their baby-strollers, Victorians and Golden Age Buffalonians drifted between the bucolic spaces with ease on those glorious summer Sundays.

Broad and tranquil parkways connected Delaware Park with The Parade (today's Martin Luther King Park) and The Front, which we call today Front Park. Calvert Vaux designed the park's original buildings and structures. Just about all of them were made in 1875 and keyed to blending with the landscape. He and Olmsted always left room,

Figure: 62

Figure: 63

though, for one outlier–"a whimsy," meaning one thing that didn't fit.

Little is left today of any of Vaux's work in Buffalo. His boathouse lasted only to 1900. "The Farmstead" had included a home for the park superintendent, plus barns and outbuildings. The Buffalo Zoo took them down for a parking lot in 1950. People can't even remember when their "whimsy" fell, the pagoda-like gazebo called "the Spire House." It was sometime between 1924 and 1951.

Vaux also designed some elaborate covered seats to shelter park users waiting for boat rides on the lake (lost between 1917 and 1951). His Gala Water Bridge at the western end of the park lake was replaced in 1890 and again in 1901. A big stone viaduct that crossed today's Delaware Avenue has been reconstructed three times at last count.

In the early 1900s somebody thought the sculpted meadow might make a nice golf course, and they laid out a nine-holer. In

1930 they finished the deal with an 18-holer. It's really fun out there if you're a golfer. Take a vision-trip and you risk getting hit by a ball. You will surely piss off the players.

The worst blast of idiocy into Olmsted's design came in the early 1960s. State planner Robert Moses took a look at a sacred park and saw little but vacant space. Let that be a lesson against urbanites deciding what everybody else ought to do. They torched a thriving neighborhood along Humboldt Parkway, once listed among the nation's most elegant streets. The construction even f-d with the park lake, turning it into a basic open sewer that festered in the back yard of the Buffalo History Museum into the 1980s. Then of course, there was an expensive cleanup.

———

My First Nations contacts tell me that the entire region of Delaware Park and Forest Lawn was the site of a rambling clash between The Six Nations Confederacy and the Kahquas (the "Neutral" Nation). I've heard it said that there may have been up to seven burial mounds and earthworks here, one of them a tumulus to the battle-

Figure: 65

Figure: 64

dead. I've never seen it confirmed by the archaeologists, and it would take one to spot an artificial mound after that many centuries of inattention. This does raise the possibility that today's cemetery could be on an ancient necropolis, a holy "city of the dead" like people say of the Spiritualist community of Lily Dale in Cassadaga, NY. It is not uncommon for societies to reuse earlier sites to the same purpose. It happened all over Europe.

Delaware Park and Forest Lawn were once part of Justice Granger's big farm and used for a U.S. Army encampment during the brutal winter of 1812-1813. At least 300 soldiers and militiamen died of a dreaded respiratory complaint called "camp fever" while here at the wet, windswept, and aptly-named Flint Hill. Most of them were relocated and buried in a softer section of the golf course by their own stone monument.

The Third Battle of Scajaquada Creek (August, 1814) was fought here, too. A sprawling affair, it moved along the banks of the creek as a robust force of British tried to cross and close with a smaller force of sharpshooting bluecoats.

First set up by attorney Charles Clarke in 1849, Forest Lawn Cemetery seems to have no single designer. It is surely inspired by one of the world's most famous burying-grounds, Père-Lachais in Paris, designed to incorporate a balance of nature and art. Forest Lawn was augmented in the 1870s by a transfusion of all the city's other burials, surely in perfect order… (You know how much fun it is digging those six-foot-deep holes in the

Opposite Page - Figure: 66

44

ground.) In fact, a lot of the city's "haunted zones" surround these allegedly emptied old graveyards. Our First Nations friends would say that the relocation screws things up at both ends. Graveless, nameless, and dishonored burials everywhere have led to folklore. No wonder there's a few ghosts at Forest Lawn!

Forest Lawn does feature private memorials, many of them Classical-style sculptures designed by architects including Richard Upjohn, Frank Lloyd Wright, E. B. Green, and Stanford White. It also hosts row upon row of the anonymous dead from the 1812 war. As if the dead seek remembrance, Forest Lawn seems blessed with a full quiver of apparitions.

Cemetery workers talk about a phantom car, one that on several occasions has led security on an unsuccessful pursuit through the winding roads. They spot its antique headlights after the gates have been chained for the night and chase after it. During one 1980s pursuit, its 1940s-style taillights seemed to grin at them like a Jack-o-lantern. Then it disappeared.

There's a book to be written about apparition-forms in the Northeast, though I doubt I will write it. Surely the message of the pattern, could one ever be derived, says something to and about the human unconscious. Like actors making cameos, some familiar patterns emerge at Forest Lawn.

The Little Girl Ghost is surely the most common ghostly archetype in the upstate. I abbreviate it in my notes when taking a report: LGG. One of Forest Lawn's twilight spooks, the wightly waif has been spotted among the stones for at least half a century by visitors and staff alike. Barefoot, white-gowned, and pathetic, Forest Lawn's LGG may be a little more interesting than the average. This one looks so real that people worry about her, alone, a lost child, and with darkness coming.

A ghostly girl has been spotted near the S-curve on Delaware and the Delaware Avenue entrance to the cemetery. At least one sighting was reported to the police in the 1950s as a Vanishing Hitchhiker–another generally female apparition most often associated with roads leading to or from burying grounds. It's different from your ordinary ghost, since it sometimes speaks and interacts–minimally–and gives a few signs of being

material. I still can't tell you what it is–if it is anything at all but "urban legend."

Anomalous Light Phenomena (ALP) is often reported at large outdoor haunts, as it is with Forest Lawn. The Six Nations folk often call these "Witch Lights" (ga'hai): energy-globes like orbs you can see with the naked eye. They are variably-colored and about the size, typically, of volleyballs. They stay generally close to the earth, five to ten feet up. Witch Lights/ALP are seen in several other Western New York graveyards, including Elmlawn in Tonawanda, Guernsey Hollow in Frewsburg, the Reist Street cemetery in Williamsville, Mt. Hope in Rochester, and Goodleberg (shudder!) in Wales. Six Nations folk think of them as either the tools or the astral forms of witches.

"The White Lady"–what folklorists call the adult woman ghost–is nearly everywhere in New York State. She's not always in white garb nor is she presumed to be Caucasian, but the name has taken hold. Forest Lawn's version comes with a back story. She's rumored to be a widow grieving one of the local war dead–who could even be manifesting as small groups of shadowy people.

Figure: 67

46

The Old Chief is another common New York apparition-form. They call Forest Lawn's version, "Red Jacket," probably because of that magnificent monument to the Seneca statesman by the Delaware gate of Forest Lawn. There should be no reason, though, for Red Jacket to show up here. He never wanted to rest in a white cemetery, and no Seneca believes his bones lie under that heroic statue. ("We gave them dog bones," one Elder told me of the time when the whites decided the great Seneca, then half a century dead, was worth honoring and came to the Cattaraugus to pick up his already-once-displaced remains.) It's hard for most whites to register the depth of feeling First Nations folk tend to have for burial-places.

You get a lot of these Old Soldier Ghosts, too, along the Niagara. I've even heard of a few redcoats in Buffalo that could be flashbacks to the city's 1813 burning. It's logical to expect an Old Soldier or two among the hundreds of war-victims at Forest Lawn. I have to steer clear of 1812-era tangents, but speaking of errant soldier-ghosts and secret graves, one of the most interesting here is that of Joseph Willcocks, a roughriding War of 1812 guerrilla shot dead outside Fort Erie in August, 1814. I know a historian who claims to be sure of the resting spot of "Canada's Benedict Arnold." He's keeping it close to the vest. If anyone else knew which one it was, the grave of the Maple Leaf nation's number one turncoat would be a cross-border beer-rental-return-site after Leafs-Sabres games.

———

These open spaces tend to get fewer stories than the clustered ones, and the Park's tales are less vivid than those of the sublime cemetery. The expressway, too, might wake the dead, but it would not encourage them to appear. Most of the apparitions I hear reported of Delaware Park are of the Old Soldier variety. Golfers,

runners, and dog-walkers in the eastern sections of Delaware Park report groups of eerie figures at dawn and dusk at the edges of the thin verdure that flanks parts of the course. Could they be the forms of patrolling soldiers, visible only in the slanting light? Several of my witnesses to this effect were standing near the mass grave of the 300.

Oddest of all, I've heard of two suspected possession cases at homes in the general region of Flint Hill. These extremely rare events are very personal to families and bitterly hard to research. They should have little or no connection to the wartime past of the region unless an occult malaise permeates any area soaked in tragedy. Those educated in the voodoo and "root magic" traditions that still thrive in Buffalo would tell us that sites over bones and accoutrements might have occult power and that unsettled "spirits" might use it to make their re-entrance into the world. Battle-ground, burial-ground, monument-ground, all landscaped to invoke vision… What wonder there's energy here?

———

It should be pointed out that the Pan-American Exposition of 1901 chewed into Delaware park, too, particularly from the north. The expressway cuts it up and makes it feel a long way off.

The Pan-Am was a fantasy-land of temporary buildings. Today's Buffalo History Museum is the only survivor. It has to be considered a Park building, and I have a modest file of reports from it for which I don't think I'd finger Olmsted and his landscaping. Most of them concern the presence and handling of First Nations artifacts. Don't forget that artifacts, too, are thought to be able to gather orenda–the Iroquoian "Force" (a la *Star Wars*)–and when they aren't handled right, you can get actups. Ours is far from the only Northeastern museum to

notice this.

Another Park site on the south side of Hoyt Lake is the Marcy Casino. Calvert Vaux's original boat house was constructed here in 1874 but lost to a fire in 1900. The three-story building we see today was rebuilt for the Pan-Am along a design by E.B. Green. Originally called The Delaware Park Casino, it was renamed in honor of Delaware District Councilman William Marcy, Jr. The top floor is a restaurant today called The Terrace.

In 2014 I interviewed an exuberant bar manager who gave me a string of ghostly stories about this Casino. The staff, too, consider the place creepy. Nobody wants to be the last to leave. I've heard of no dramatic apparitions, though. Most of the talk concerns the typical SPOTUK, my acronym for that very common pattern, "Spooky Phenomena of the Usual Kind." That means electrical effects, unexplained sounds, relocated small objects, darting shadows, funky moving forms… The place does have a lot of glass, with many light-effects and reflections that could create the impression of apparitions. You can decide for yourself if any of them are supernatural. You cannot disagree that there is folklore.

I know this is a piece about Olmsted's layout, but this Rose Garden (1917) deserves a look, even though we can tribute Olmsted for it only indirectly. The work of City Hall's parks department, it seems to be based on the

design of a landscape architect from Cleveland, A. D. Taylor (1883-1951). Taylor had worked for Warren Manning (1860-1938), who had worked under Olmsted.

My crude endeavors with google maps and Photoshop have led me to believe that Marcy Casino has the footprint of the Golden Rectangle. There could be some geometric interplay at work between the Casino and the Rose Garden, too. The Garden's pathways appear to make a pair of squares whose sides equal the length of the Casino, depending upon the points you pick to measure. For what it's worth, I've interviewed people who have had inexplicable trance-moments in the Rose Garden at off-times of the year–like a bleak winter afternoon or a dripping May one–so maybe the form is there and has some effect upon mood.

While we hail him for his work in Buffalo, Calvert Vaux has fallen into Olmsted's shadow. He was the Andrew Ridgeley of Wham! He was the Oates of Hall and Oates. A word needs to be said about him here.

Many architects form partnerships. In some of them, the businessperson is the glue and the artist is the one people remember. Vaux and Olmsted were different. Vaux's precise role in these sculpted landscapes was to design the man-made features–boathouses, gazebos, bridges, and the like–that had to be *right there*, and "just so." These were the ornaments to the Olmsted canvas like the decorative icons of Louis Sullivan, John Wade, and James Johnson were onto Buffalo buildings. Vaux shared Olmsted's belief that architecture came in second to Nature. Nature had "baked the cake." The landscape artist smoothed the frosting. The bridges and pagodas of partner-architects like Vaux set the cherry atop it. Vaux might have been the only architect who could have worked so closely with the mature Olmsted.

Maybe as a symbol of his retiring nature, Vaux's death, too, was a mystery. One November morning in 1895 he went for a walk in Brooklyn and was last spotted alive stepping onto a pier at Bath Beach Park. He was quickly reported as missing. His body was found the next day in the water at the foot of 17th Street. He had been a frailer-by-the-day 70-year old, and there were no overt signs of foul play. Still, toppling off of a pier like that seemed to everyone a strange end.

———

In my 20s and 30s–until I blew out my ankle–I used to play the Buffalo Municipal Public Parks Tennis Tournament, aka "the MUNY." I got into some late rounds in singles but never won any of the divisions. I won a number of doubles events, which I attribute to selecting good partners.

Most of the matches were on the McMillan courts along the Scajaquada Expressway, and I remember that it took time–years–to adjust to the traffic that roared and hurled ten feet behind me when I served or returned from the south side. I had to take it like the hoots and taunts of a crowd in a gladiatorial arena. Still, as if Olmsted's power could be detected even then, it always felt to me like there was something a little sacramental at "Buffalo's Wimbledon." If I won, it was a triumph in the Colosseum. If I lost, as mad as I usually was, it was a noble sacrifice, "the good fight" waged without quarter asked or given. I felt an unusual sense of audience. I wonder if even then I sensed what I know now.

I keep referring to that jazz solo whose melody is so intricate that only the rare hearer can pick it. Even if I could interpret it for myself, Olmsted's visual message would be impossible to put into words. It was not meant for the frontal cortex, for language. It was meant to speak to other parts of the mind–and all the spirit. It's fainter now at "The Park," but surely something of it holds.

———

Burlington, VT, and Boulder, CO, both have famous urban walking malls. The broad lanes are cut off from motor vehicles and hence give us latitude to ornament them with statues and stonework, and a line of discordant sculptures runs down the core of either. Some are simple natural things like trees and boulders, presented like works of art. Some are representative stone and metal statues. Some are fairly classic architectural features like columns and arches. Some are experimental and abstract, things like you might find at a gallery of Modern Art.

This line of fixtures reminds me of the Surrealist painting of the mismatched items simply posted–or posing–on a long and receding road in a blank natural environment. Animals, artifacts, and instruments were simply situated, as if waiting for the viewer to make their meaning. Its sheer absurdity made made me think Terry Gilliam's Time Bandits had shot through in a haste, lightening their load and leaving a trail of pilfered objects–or else a weight-shedding wagon train had dropped the leftovers of a yard sale onto the track Noah's ark had seeded with a few placid, confused animals.

Someone once decided to study video surveillance and

Figure: 71

see which type of image the mall-urchins preferred by their flocking habits. Overwhelmingly they chose to gather around the natural forms, the trees and stoneworks, or the classic representative ones. It was as if those images were more comforting to the psyche. Even the skate punks and street folk–who would seem to be anti-classic rebels–gravitated to the natural, as if something could be within all of us that responds to it. Let that be a testament against the stereotype, as well as to the power of the natural.

3

The Cave of Polyphemus

Henry Hobson Richardson (1838-1886)
The Buffalo Psychiatric Center (1871)
444 Forest Avenue, Buffalo

Never forget how young we Americans are, as a nation and as a culture, compared to so many in the world. We were younger still in days that seem historic to us. We started as a coastal, then frontier nation. We had few academies and less of the sort of leisure time that enables such outwardly unnecessary activities as the arts. The American arts had to earn their esteem next to those of Europe, and it was not an immediate process. The Hudson River painters, the Transcendentalist philosophers, and authors like Mark Twain, perhaps our Chaucer, and Walt Whitman–the American Wordsworth, if we have one–surged forward to claw respect from crusty hearts. About the time of the American Civil War some French scholar I cannot name for you was the first to observe that the United States had a significant tradition of literature ready to stand with those of the Old World. (He also noted that we tended to be rough-edged, anti-academic, and a bit rebellious.) The first American to really crush it in architecture is the subject of this piece, one who was, according to the art historian John Russell, "One of the great unfinished poems of American cultural history."

Henry Hobson Richardson (1838-1886) spent his early life in Louisiana on the family plantation. He had the genes for greatness if there is such a thing. His mother's grandfather Joseph Priestley was the scientist who discovered oxygen, as well as soda water and the pencil eraser. A stutter kept young Henry out of West Point and the military and drove him toward Harvard and civil engineering. No engineer, he found, he drifted into architecture and graduated, more distinguished as a partier than a scholar. "Fez" Richardson, as his buddies called him, had hipster friends who liked British and Classical themes: Hasty Pudding, Porcellian clubs, the Pierian Sodality. Those contacts would serve him well.

Richardson was at the École des Beaux-Arts when the American Civil War commenced. No fan of slavery, he rode the war out in Paris. He was no fan of neoclassicism, either, which to him meant evoking Greek and Roman architectural patterns with little modification. To Richardson and a number of his peers, it was silly to free-snatch classical motifs for buildings–and a world!–the Greeks and Romans had never imagined.

Richardson opened his architectural practice in New York on May Day, 1866. A year later he entered a partnership with Charles Dexter Gambrill (1834-1880) with whom he had an arrangement a bit like that of some successful

Figure: 73

Figure: 74

Figure: 75

unions we'll see ahead. Gambrill managed the business side of things and Richardson developed the designs.

In the post-Civil War years, the United States was undergoing a phase of admiration for two architectural styles: Gothic Revival (English) which everyone knows from the Dracula movies; and Second Empire (French) that we in Buffalo may see in The Mansion on Delaware, AKA, "the Sternberg Mansion" or "the Trubee House." Richardson's early work doesn't step too far out of the pack. He was good, but he wasn't *Richardson*. In 1872 he took a major step forward: He won the contest to design the mammoth Trinity Episcopal Church in Boston. He was suddenly one of the most sought-after architects in the United States.

If a year could be said to mark the point at which Richardson hit stride, it might be 1878. In three projects–Sever Hall in Cambridge, MA, the Ames Monument in Wyoming, and the Crane Library in Quincy, MA–Richardson started streamlining. The statements of his buildings were made in basic forms, as well as through the materials themselves, typically brick, stone, or shingles. This was his signature style, "Richardsonian Romanesque."

By 1882 Richardson had streamlined his team approach, too. He gave sketches to his draftsmen to develop as drawings. An old hand among them could steer each design. When ground was broken, this sidekick could supervise, freeing Richardson of the need to be quite so hands-on and boot-ready. Because of this division of labor, he could focus on what he was good at and handle a lot more business. He had too much anyway. By then he was one of the top architects in the Western world.

One of his clients, John Glessner of Chicago, wrote that Richardson had "supreme confidence in his own powers." That sort of man, continued Glessner, "never is envious or critical of others." Even in what mattered most to him–his art–Richardson could suffer and even nurture the less gifted. Some of Richardson's proteges are names in their own right, and five are well represented in Buffalo. Stanford White and Charles Follen McKim went on to form the massively successful McKim, Mead, and White. Daniel Burnham developed not only Buffalo's Ellicott Square Building but a nearly Olmsted-ian style of city planning for Chicago that anticipated rapid expansion. Andrew Jackson Warner and Louis Sullivan lie ahead.

Figure: 76

Everyone who knew Richardson thought of him as a merry man. He was wont to jest that two of his apprentices, McKim and Burnham, took on the hardest problems that ever confronted men in their profession: They designed buildings for their future fathers-in-law, inviting the risk of lifelong criticism.

That wit may live for us as long as Richardson's buildings. In an astonishing paper on Richardson's use of the Golden Section, the Yale-trained architect Richard L. Brown shows us that Richardson has quite the jest with Austin Hall.

Figure: 77

The frieze of the original Harvard Law School building is inscribed with King James Bible-esque words of legal wisdom. ("And thou shalt teach them the way wherein they must walk and the work that they must do.") People have been passing under it for 140 years. Yet the figures carved into the stone around the entrance seem comically confused. They could be mocking the profession taught within.

Two-headed, "Which way did he go?" eagles stand back to back, seeming to look everywhere and see nothing. Animals chase their own tails, dragons are leashed together in a pointless tug-of-war, snakes entangle human figures, and absurd little faces take expressions, a la Mr. Brown, that "would not be complimentary to anyone." (Maybe the Three Stooges.) The plaque holding Richardson's monogram is mounted just under a dragonlike being sinking fangs into its own fanny with the expression of a puppy tugging on a toy. Posted at the entrance of a law school, it all suggests that Richardson was having some fun with the profession taught within. Richard Brown is more direct: "All the plaques, trim, and downspouts make lawyers look like idiots."

That easy nature seems to have tempered the perfectionism we'll see to come in Sullivan and Wright. Still, Richardson's attitude might well be summed up in a line attributed to him: "Let me but have time to finish (big projects in) Pittsburgh and I should be content without another day." It seems to state the compulsion for expression that we usually associate with poets, painters, or composers. How sad it is to demolish a structure that might have been the cry of a soul!

Also regrettable is the fact that Richardson was not a healthy man. More than most of us he loved good food and drink. Large by 30, he was soon after ponderous–six feet and 350 pounds. He suffered from Bright's disease, a renal disorder that could be of genetic origin. In his early

Figure: 78

40s he met with a specialist, Sir William Gull, who advised him that nothing could be improved by overwork. Richardson went back to his usual pace when he got home. He left us at 47, and rests today in Walnut Hill Cemetery, not far from where he had lived in Brookline, MA. One only wonders what he would have accomplished with more years. The length of Frank Lloyd Wright's working career tripled that of Richardson.

Richardson had a huge income but left his widow and five children with little. He seems to have been a poor money manager. With Richardson, according to Phillips Brooks, "His life passed into his buildings by ways too subtle for himself to understand." Maybe that was why he didn't keep his house in order: His being went into every other one he made.

————

Romanesque architecture is castle-like. It's inspired by the hardy features–parapets, turrets, and thick walls–of Medieval fortresses, specifically those of Spain, Italy, and France. Most Romanesque buildings look like they are meant to withstand sieges–or earthquakes. They tend to lack ornament, too. They make their statements with big shapes. Almost all Richardson buildings have some of the features of castles, but Richardson's Romanesque was updated, more or less a softening of Gothic architecture, giving curves and flow you don't see in many forts.

Next to our modernist architecture and strip malls, anything done by Richardson looks pretty classic. It's hard for us to feel the impact of how radical his vision was. When Richardson started proposing the blend of Renaissance and Romanesque that would come to be named after him, his outraged peer Richard Morris Hunt found it "absolutely inharmonious" and "a direct antagonism to the received rules of art." Hunt was a traditionalist. He hadn't seen eye to eye with Richardson's buddy Olmsted, either. Hunt had designed some grand classical entrances to Central Park that for Olmsted and Vaux was missing the point of a retreat–making "natural eloquence" play second fiddle to "architectural grandiloquence," as Hugh Howard summarizes.

Even at his popular peak, Richardson's work could affront his peers. His Ames Gate Lodge in North Easton, MA–at first glance an inhabitable viaduct–took more than one of his contemporaries by utter storm. "An extraordinary

Figure: 79

piece of architectural athleticism," wrote the Boston architect Henry Van Brunt of it, "a specimen of boisterous Titanic gamboling… which might have been piled up by a Cyclops." For novelist and historian Henry Adams it seemed "the cave of Polyphemus," the one-eyed giant who so beleaguered Homer's Odysseus. To me it looks like someone offered an outcrop to be converted into living-space and a pack of Tolkien's dwarves had obliged. It's truly beautiful, though…unusual.

I forgive Richardson's contemporaries. Great art tends to prod, not soothe, its time. Those entrenched in the status quo aren't ready for it. Ah, even Shakespeare had his critics. So did Keats, like that one who could never quite wrap his head around that "beaker full of the warm South."

Richardson is well represented on the Niagara. He built a house in Buffalo for William Dorsheimer, which still stands at 434-438 Delaware. Less fortunate was the Gratwick House at 776 Delaware. That demolition you can't blame on the politicians or the inattention thereof.

Opposite Page - Figure: 80

Figure: 81

Figure: 82

Neighbors on each side figured they'd like a bit more lawn. They bought and leveled the Gratwick in 1919. Got us a damn fine parking lot there today.

Two examples of Richardson's Niagara Frontier work may be indirect–or uncertain. Richardson's railroad station in Auburndale, MA, was acknowledged a masterpiece and described as "the best he ever built." It was demolished in the 1960s to make way for the Massachusetts Turnpike, whose planners of course could not possibly have budged its route a few feet either way–or made use of a stylish rest stop. An exact replica of Richardson's station was built in 1911 in Orchard Park. It's still there–and it gets a few ghost stories.

And there's a house in East Aurora, "Rushing Waters," overlooking the Cazenovia Creek along The Big Tree Road that some say was Richardson's design. It's Romanesque, but done in his "shingle" style, with a glorious Normanesque tower whose walls bear zodiacal bas-reliefs. It's not conclusive that no one remembers it

as Richardson's. In those days not everybody made a lasting note of who an architect was, at least when it was a private home. The architect, anyway, is proverbially the most unseen of artists. Rushing Waters' original owner was banker-painter William Caryl Cornwell (1851-1932), a Buffalo Club member at the time Richardson was hanging out there.

———

Richardson influenced generations of architects. Both Louis Sullivan and Frank Lloyd Wright found themselves bespelled with the rough materials and massy qualities of Richardsonian structures. Ah, no one could make the blocky beautiful quite like "Fez." The former State Asylum for the Insane on Forest Avenue in Buffalo is merely one of the most obvious. It was also the debut of the style named for Richardson –and the biggest project of his career.

Medina red sandstone makes most of today's Buffalo Psychiatric Center. It's a common building material in the

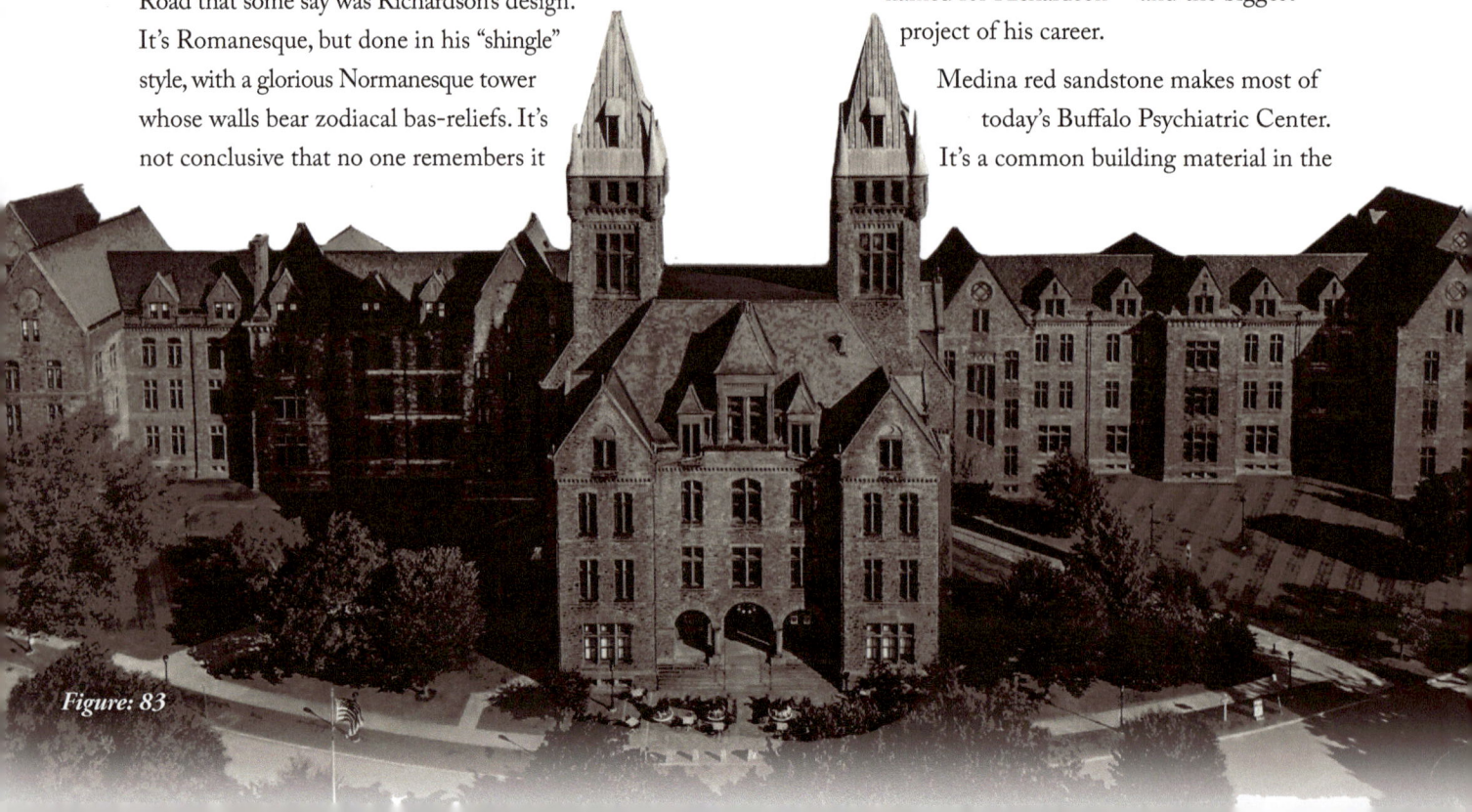

Figure: 83

region. You may notice that many of the wards–those less ornate flanking buildings–are of red brick. They had to cut corners. A recession struck during the long construction.

"Buffalonians like to imagine all kinds of torture taking place in its dramatic twin towers," notes the astute Buffalo author and historian Cynthia van Ness. Actually, the Buffalo Asylum was a big break from the past and a humanitarian advance in the treatment of the mentally ill. These patients were not warehoused. They were protected. They were given *asylum* from the pressures of their former lives. They had private rooms, indoor plumbing, and sunny, airy circumstances (at least when the Niagara was sunny). These were comforts found in few Buffalo homes of the day.

Everything down to the landscaping was meant to provide the peaceful circumstances thought to be so influential in the cure of mental and emotional complaints. Frederick Law Olmsted came in to make a tag-team of it with Richardson. Walking the park-like grounds and sculpted paths was soothing and enlightening. Anyone who's ever thoughtfully walked a labyrinth will know what I mean. Farming the fields and working in the gardens would have been considered exercises in zen-like transcendence.

Once Olmsted's plantings were in place, the potentially gloomy monument betrayed "no air of incarceration," according to Hugh Howard. Under his hand the entrance to the Administration Building looked more like that to a zoo or a botanical garden. Much like Wright and Richardson with building materials, Olmsted stayed as indigenous as he could with trees and flowers.

———

I see symbolism in a general way at the popularly called "Psych Center." The site's most distinctive feature, those witch-hat towers at the Administration Building /Richardson Hotel, make for the most dramatic night-landscape in our city. I wonder if they could have been the models for those on London's Tower Bridge (1886-1894). And that structure is the ceremonial bridge or gateway

Figure: 84

between the occupants it was designed to nurture and the outer world, the urban environment of the city Buffalo toward its south. To its north, in the day, was nothing but fields, woods, and creek.

The form of the complex, too, I find symbolic. The flattened V of the original Asylum–five buildings to each side of the Administration Building–featured long rambling wings arranged *en echelon* (staggered), likened to a skien of geese in flight. The point was ensuring that none of the buildings blocked any other from getting air and light. It was meant to promote privacy and comfort for the patients.

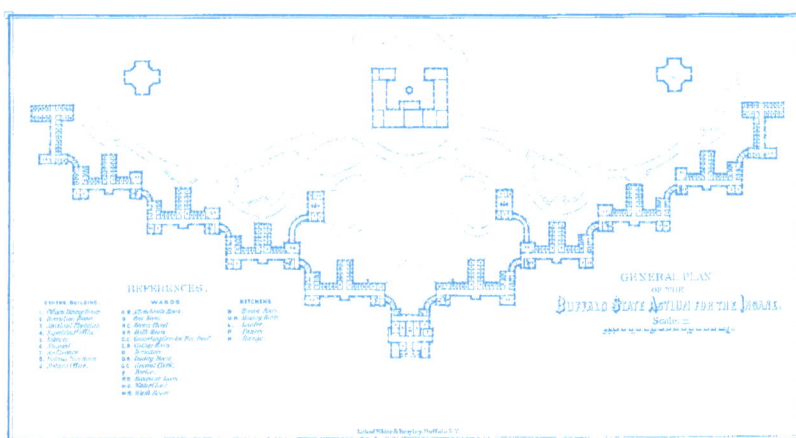

Figure: 85

Richardson's Asylum followed the general plan of Thomas Story Kirkbride (1809–1883), a Philadelphia psychiatrist who developed his designs based on a philosophy of both human compassion and a respect for nature and landscape. The typical Kirkbride footprint has also been likened to the wings of a bat, rousing unfortunate speculation about the source of one of our synonyms for "crazy" (i. e., "bats"). The central axis to our Buffalo building inclines just a bit west of due north which gets us again suspecting archaeoastronomy. The avowed reason for the alignment was that Richardson wanted to give his structure the maximum exposure to natural sunlight, which meant to the southern horizon. Yet we remember Ellicott's 15° east-of-north alignment and its parallels to the ancient Meso-city Teotihuacan. If the Richardson Complex's alignment was 15° west of true north, I might regard it as a deliberate response to Old Joe Ellicott, whose work Richardson and Olmsted were known to have admired. It does not seem to be such a tribute. The Richardson's alignment looks to me to be 19° west of due north, which isn't ringing any esoteric bells. Maybe someone else can find a connection.

While I don't know that Richardson ever used the term "organic architecture"–incorporating structure to site–he surely anticipated the concept. Some of his buildings like the Ames Gate Lodge look to be such natural features that they could have grown out of the ground. When surveying his Buffalo site, Richardson noticed several ravines running like the ridge, east and west on the proposed footprint of the 2200-foot wide building. Thinking interior transport might be useful, he adapted them into subways big enough for wheeled vehicles.

Symbolism of a basic–non-esoteric–type is surely made by the form of the Complex on its landscape. Its outline makes a protective arc, curving as if to let stressful forces break around it like a bulwark against the cluttered energies of the city to its south. It's also a bow, though, with a nock–those two intriguing towers–at the Administration Building. The imaginary arrow, the human flow, is aimed at the city core. That figures. This Administration Building is the site of the entry and the sally-back of those the place hoped to welcome and then discharge. It all suggests the latent power to receive and protect its temporary guests and then launch them back into the urban society when the nurturing archer is ready to release the shaft. Such a journey was hoped for each patient.

———

Richardson wrote next to nothing about his work. As a long time teacher, I almost wonder if he could have been a brother to my dyslexic students, for most of whom writing was anathema. He had some of their earmarks. He had wondrous social gifts, as do many of them. His visual-spatial awareness was off the charts. He could play chess in his head without seeing a board. And there was that youthful stutter to be remembered.

What signs are there that he meant to fashion "occult" architecture that might heighten the mystical experience? There's a simple answer: He didn't need to mean to. The architectural styles that tend to produce supernatural folklore weren't occult in the 19th century, merely arcane. Esoteric. Revivalist. Anyone who attended the École in Richardson's day would be exposed to little else.

Richardson was cagey enough to think for himself. His personal library, though, showed influences. Richardson seems to have collected everything John Ruskin and Eugène Emmanuel Viollet-le-Duc wrote. Either one is significant in any discussion of medievalesque/occult architecture. Ruskin, "the Great Victorian," was the philosophical father of the medieval-revival Arts & Crafts Movement that so marked its age–and East Aurora's Roycroft. Viollet-le-Duc went to great lengths to promote the use of the Egyptian Triangle.

———

Richard L. Brown had long been fascinated by a plaque at Harvard's Austin Hall, the one holding Richardson's monogram next to the dragon auto-chomping ass. In a flash the key to a visual puzzle revealed itself to him. That plaque was a virtual Rosetta stone toward understanding the proportioning of the whole structure. It is pictured here.

"By using his proportions to relate the largest idea down to the smallest detail," writes Brown, "Richardson created a unifying link throughout the structure… Although Richardson almost always used the Golden Section proportions, within the Golden Section he developed for each building its own sequence of proportions that give each building its own rhythm and continuity." Richardson didn't write about his system. He left roadmaps. One of them was that plaque at Austin Hall.

It has an appealing look quite common for forms that embody sacred shape. It holds imagery, too: Richardson's compressed initials, with some Masonic square-and-

Figure: 86

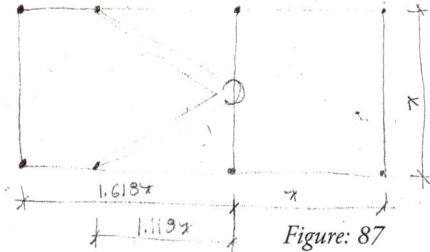

Figure: 87

Figure: 88

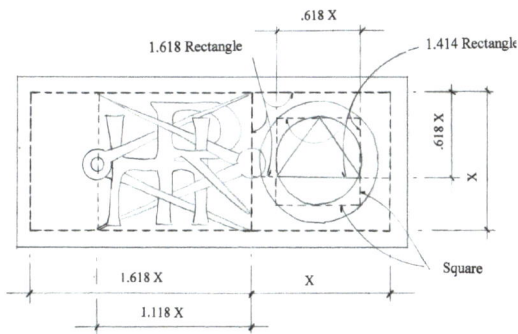

Figure: 89

Figure: 90

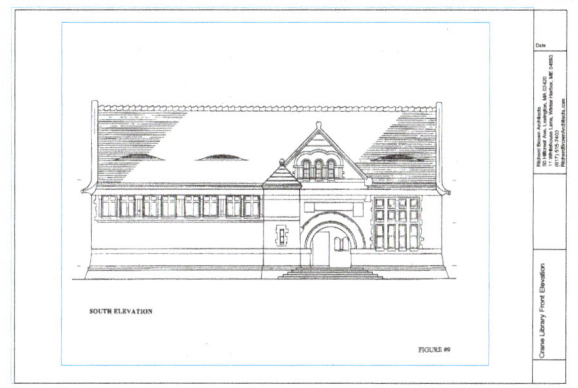

Figure: 91

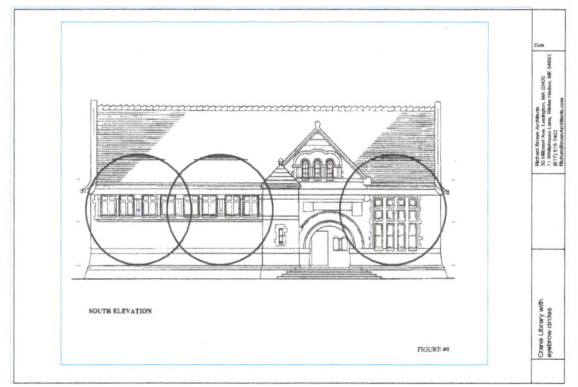

Figure: 92

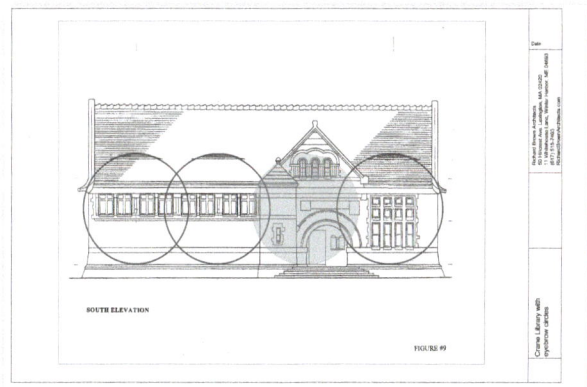

Figure: 93

compass shapes and a Celtic-style knot enfolding a triangle.

In this plaque Brown discovered four basic shapes used commonly by Richardson: the square; the Golden Rectangle; and two spins of the Golden Rectangle made by adding parts, like a half of the square or another small Golden Shape. (I've often wondered if the facades of some of Buffalo's fine buildings like the Birge Mansion might have been made of overlapping but identical Golden Rectangles. Now that I know it may not be that rare, you may see me out there with my tape measure!)

"Richardson is really fascinating when it comes to hidden messages," writes Richard Brown. Since many Richardson buildings are imponderably vast, Brown picked a manageable one for a test case. He found the Crane Library in Quincy, MA, surreally integrated. Not only were there layers of superimposed forms in the design of doors and windows, but virtually every feature on every level and dimension responded to the original motif. It was almost fractal, yet even more poetic.

"The design of the fireplace and the windowpanes are related to the design of the front elevation," notes Brown. "The process that designs the plan is the same process that designs the doorknob." One striking example is a trio of lunettes –eyebrow-like forms that in this case are windows– on the front facade. They match the arcs of three big imaginary circles that fit perfectly within the geometric theme. Notice the vesica piscis design formed by the two to the left. Notice in the third sketch my imposition of a shadow-circle that, doubtless, we're also intended to imagine.

Figure: 94

Richardson held his buildings together, according to Brown, "by creating a common rhythm in all the forms, objects, and spaces." This intricate concept Brown calls, "the sequence of proportions." It hides invisibly, one suspects, in every surviving Richardsonian structure. It was undeniably an expression of "organic architecture" for which Louis Sullivan and then Frank Lloyd Wright came to be known. As every cell of a living being is programmed with its distinctive DNA, so some of these structures are integrated by the architect's original plan, thus echoing the Creation. Maybe that is what the G in the Masonic square-and-compass symbol stands for after all: God.

———

You'd think Richardson's diagrams would be everywhere, but it's not always easy to get a look at the plans of many important buildings. Some have never been digitized. Some are on microfilm and buried in libraries–like Richardson's at Harvard. Others have been discarded. That's a funny way to treat American masters, but we're back again to the image of the invisible architect. In Shakespeare's day they didn't consider the script of a play to be anything special. For them the stage was a live art like a dance. I can only list a few of the things I see at the Buffalo masterpiece.

Dr. Kirkbride had a general plan for his hospitals, but the immediate design was surely Richardson's. The overall plan of the Buffalo complex from above hints at some geometrical pattern. There are suggestions that the Golden Rectangle or a spin of it might have been evoked. Notice, too, those two structures to the north like perfectly balanced Maltese crosses twinkling like stars or eyes above the smile of the bow. They are gone today, but they were marked to be greenhouses, and surely that's what they were.

Another curiosity needs to be addressed, and it hides in plain sight a hundred feet north of the Administration Building. It doesn't appear in Richardson's original diagrams, and you can walk right by it and never notice it, like I did in April, 2024. Then you go to the Google maps and wonder how you could have missed it. Big enough to be a parking lot or all left of a lost building, it's basically a big, shallow, concrete-walled box with no lid to it. Its cross-shaped outline instantly suggests sacred design.

Maybe this cruciform plot is what seeded the rumor of an old cemetery that once served as a resting place for late patients. It figures that mortality within the Buffalo Asylum could have been higher than that outside. Many patients came to it stressed and lonely and already ill. Still, we have to lay the rumor of an indigents' graveyard to rest. This space was once that of a greenhouse, and one built in 1888, two years after Richardson's death. It was taken down and its footprint is all that was left. A section of one of the Lackawanna cemeteries might have served several Buffalo hospitals, anyway, as the Potter's Field, as a beggars' burial ground is often called.

The Administration Building is the most distinctive structure at the Asylum. Its footprint looks to be a square, and one that might relate to shadow-form established around it with other buildings.

The sketch I have of the front elevation appears to show the overall form of the Golden Rectangle from the base to the tip of the towers. Two smaller Golden Rectangles stood by each other seem to fit from the base to the

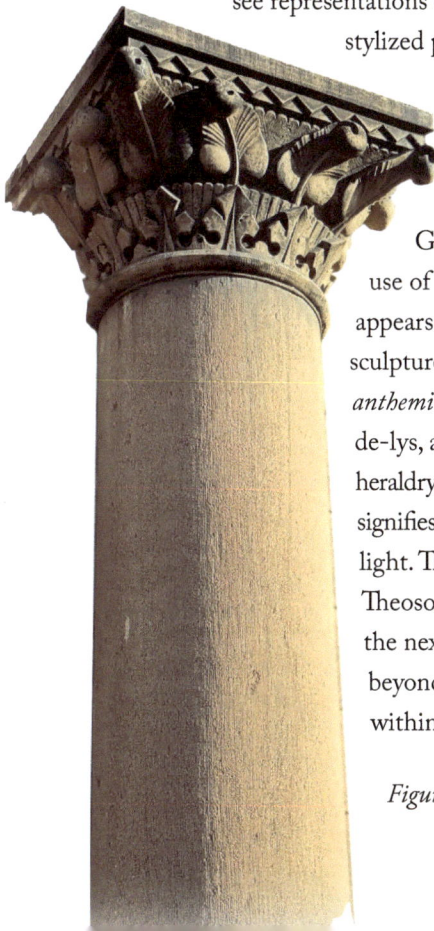

roofline. It would be logical to expect patterns like double-squares and smaller Golden Rectangles to be present and expressed elsewhere like even fractal forms, but it would take a look at the plans and a scholar like Richard Brown to bring them out. Yet surely there is a design here that the mind may not register but the eye admires. You wonder at its effects on the spirit.

Occult/sacred imagery is found all over the Asylum. We see vinous, leafy images of what may be the acanthus plant, a pan-Mediterranean symbol of immortality. We see representations of the palmette, a stylized palm leaf used as a decoration in ancient Egypt. It represented life, mortality, and even divinity. The Greeks picked up the use of it, and when it appears in their art and sculpture it's called the *anthemion*. There's the fleur-de-lys, a symbol in French heraldry. A stylized lotus, it signifies life, completeness, and light. This is uplifting, even Theosophical, imagery: to the next life, to the world beyond this, to the spirit within all of us.

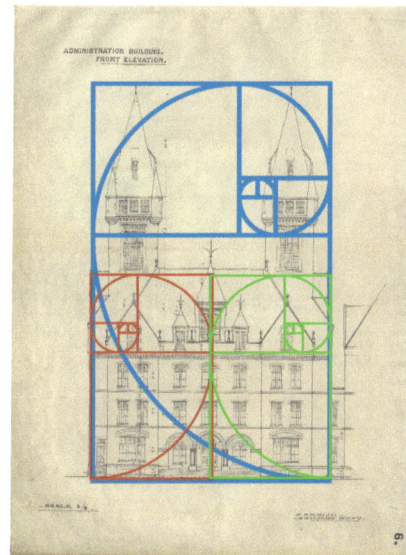

Figure: 97

One oft-repeated symbol at the Richardson is a stubby, rounded cross inside a circle, frequently in grand form. This they call "the Pierced Quatrefoil." It's very medieval-Gothic, probably symbolizing "the squared circle," the joining of the contraries, so critical to the Gnostics, the Alchemists, and other Renaissance mystics. Just look at what Blake, the British Romantic poet-painter and resurrected Gnostic, made out of the union of the opposites.

Don't forget the Administration Building's unusual cornerstone with the lettering: A.L. 5872 A.D. 1872 / SEPTEMBER 18. This a Masonic in-joke. The Freemasons have a ceremonial date for the creation of the world: 4000 BC. Thus with some of their formal inscriptions and publications, 4000 years is added to any calendar date. (The "A.L." is short for anno lucis, in Latin, "year of light," surely meaning, 'After Jesus.') It's an echo of the Jewish rabbinical tradition that the creation of the world could be given a precise date. (I hear Oct. 7, 3761 BC, is the accepted ceremonial date these days.) The Freemasons have a lot of sympathy for Jewish tradition.

Figure: 99

Those apparent crossing V's on the plaque represent the compass, the top one, and the "square," that are so significant in Masonic symbolism. While this doesn't deter speculations about Richardson's Masonic interests, it may be no direct sign of them. It may simply represent the fact that Buffalo -area Masons contributed the cornerstone–which I'd have studied closely by now if Richardson had been the one to fashion it.

———

Was Richardson a member of any occult fraternal/ philosophical society? Was he interested in a single mystical discipline? He did design the Oliver Ames Masonic Temple in North Easton, MA. Its proprietors today accept without questioning that Richardson was a member of the Lodge. Masonic historian Jason Sutton found an article in which Gerald B. Nordling referred to Richardson as, "(Bro.) Henry Hobson Richardson," which is one way Freemasons acknowledge their fellows in print. "The author seemed diligent and reliable in his research," writes Sutton, "but unfortunately I don't believe he is still alive for us to confirm where he got the information."

Neither Richardson nor Olmsted is listed among William R. Denslow's *10,000 Famous Freemasons.* Neither is Andrew Jackson Warner, though, whom we'll study

soon–and Warner was by most local accounts an active Mason in the Genesee Valley. I wonder at this book's completeness.

Images like the Masonic square and compass recur on many of Richardson's monograms and plaques. But I point out again that many people who use symbolism associated with a group are not members of it. I use symbolism all over my fiction and I'm no occultist. Richardson's age was one in which artists loved occult symbols. They had a lot to work with. I've told you about that Western system of mystical symbolism and philosophy, "the Hermetic-Cabalist tradition." And not every initiate of any society is interested in depth symbolism. For most Freemasons, the Lodge is a fraternal order.

There is the factor of those widely circulated portraits of Richardson in a monkish robe. I've heard associations with a number of occult societies, not all of them savory. (The Illuminati.) While it has been called a publicity photo emphasizing Richardson's adoption of the Romanesque/monastic style, that might be a simple explanation. It's at the least a testament of his flair for medievalism, which itself would have been equipped with *The Da Vinci Code* tendencies. There is indeed a sort of underground, pan-Western lingo of shape, form, geometry, mathematics, symbolism, and key words by which artists and architects have been talking to each other across the centuries. Dan Brown didn't make all that up. Not by a long shot.

———

To me, folklore is a matter of the human record. I have information I will never reveal because it was given to me in confidence. I have material from First Nations tradition that I won't reveal because I know it is sensitive to the traditionalists among them. Some things I won't speak or write about because they could damage families and living individuals. Asking a question about the ghostly gossip at a famous and monumental site seems like it ought to be fair game. Half the people in Buffalo told me that "the Psych Center" was a great place to look for it.

Figure: 100

Still, some of our contemporaries are on guard for any stereotyping or discrimination against… whatever you call it this decade. The alternately-saned. Mentally ill. I wonder sometimes about our current obsession with terminology–and changing it every five years.

In 1996 I was working on my first book, *Shadows of the Western Door*, and looking for folklore. Wondering what people in the building thought about it, I called the then-main line of the entity running the Richardson complex. I did not hide my purpose.

People kept shifting me up the line of extensions till I came to a supervisor who sounded like she expected a positive cancer diagnosis. I asked my question and got…a reaction.

I tried to parry with reason. Good luck. I couldn't help the speaker avoid making the reflexive connection of supernatural folklore, the joys of Victorian psychotherapy–"It was only trying to help…"–and the enduring discrimination against those in need of a time-out, no matter how long dead. I ended up assuring her that if representatives of The Richardson did not want the site to be in that book on the region's folklore, I would not include it. I did not. I would not include it now except that, with the explosion of the ghost-business on the internet and TV–and at least fifty years of ghost-breaking urban thrill-seekers–I would be the only "ghost guy" in the Northeast who doesn't get to write about it. Not only is that horse out of the barn, it's entering this year's Kentucky Derby.

———

Many factors could be involved in the Richardson's eerie prestige. While the Administration Building is today gloriously restored, there is physical mystery to other parts of the vast complex. (A brisk walk from one end to the other could take you ten minutes.) And those tunnels! It's still largely un-renovated, too. The dark spaces are cave-like and ominous. Day or night, there is significant hazard to roaming about.

These alone could have made the Richardson the dominant legend site in the city of Buffalo, a human-made realm of EHE, "exceptional human experience." Generations of Buffalo kids, 20-something thrill seekers, and amateur ghost hunters have come out of its voluminous confines with wild-stories. If I wrote up every experience I've heard I'd still believe I haven't touched a percent of what is to be had. I'll summarize.

There's the familiar SPOTUK: shadows, cold spots, heavy footsteps, and creepy sensations. Oddly, the sounds are of things people envision: bouncing balls and the squeaking wheels of antique baby carriages. The motif of "the abandoned playground" is strong here.

People report oddities and malfunctions with any sort of electrical devices in these unoccupied wings. Maybe this explains the orbs and "ectoplasm"–misty forms–they pick up on cameras. FYI, pop TV ghost hunting has altered the original meaning of "ectoplasm" to signify that smoky slime today's ghost-hunters pick up just about everywhere they shoot. The term *ectoplasm* was coined in Richardson's day to signify the presumed extra-physical substance that created the material displays of both the performance mediums of the Victorian period and the poltergeist activity that has been observed for centuries.

I've heard of no agreed-upon haunter that dominates the vast space, which is reasonable. Most seriously reported ghosts are site-specific and even room-specific. That sets off a world of speculation about ghosts in general that doesn't seem to be the point of this book on architects, sacred architecture, and folklore.

Some of the apparitions at the Richardson are those of confused-looking people in antique clothing, suggestive of former tenants. The rest come in archetypes, generic forms like you'd get all across the state: the White Lady, the Little Girl Ghost, the Shadow, the Ghost Children.

The last of them makes little sense to me. The beings presumed at root are often associated with sounds and prankish behavior. There are or once were said to be

artifacts left in parts of the building, and the kiddy-ghosts are said to love befuddling you with them. Other than the wonder of folklore and EHE at powerful sights, I don't know why child-ghosts should be expected here. This touches another nerve in the perceptive folklorist: the Little People. It calls for an aside.

Another of the great surprises I had when I started my study of the upstate paranormal was to find that intelligent, seemingly rational contemporaries would report seeing and otherwise experiencing figures I and just about everyone else thought were confined to folklore. Like fairies. Due to my interest in Western and First Nations mythologies, I was pretty well grounded on fairy-folklore when I noted this. I had never thought I would meet anyone who said they saw the real things.

While not fingering the Richardson as a Little People-site, which would be wondrous, I should mention that when witnesses do report seeing these diminutive, magical humans, the apparitions present themselves in the trappings–sounds, sights, and impish playfulness–of human children. This is just as they appear in classic folklore. The Little People, furthermore, are a rare category of apparitions. You don't get Little People reports at the average haunted house. They tend to be linked to the most unique natural wonders and the grandest human monuments. In the Old World, battlefields, forts, and sacred sites tend to get folklore of all types, including fairy-lore. It's possible that the Richardson qualifies here, too.

The old commenters noted that the Native societies built forts on high points on both sides of the Niagara. It's possible that Richardson's triumph is on or near a former monument-site, either a fort, a burial ground, or a sacred place. My First Nations friends keep the tradition that this area around the Scajaquada Creek was the scene of a sprawling pre-Columbian battle between Native societies. It may have something to do with the reputed burial mounds at Forest Lawn Cemetery. That's a short walk from the Richardson, but watch it when you hop that lovely expressway.

———

In my experience, you can interview ninety-nine people about a single site and get ten stories out of the whole.

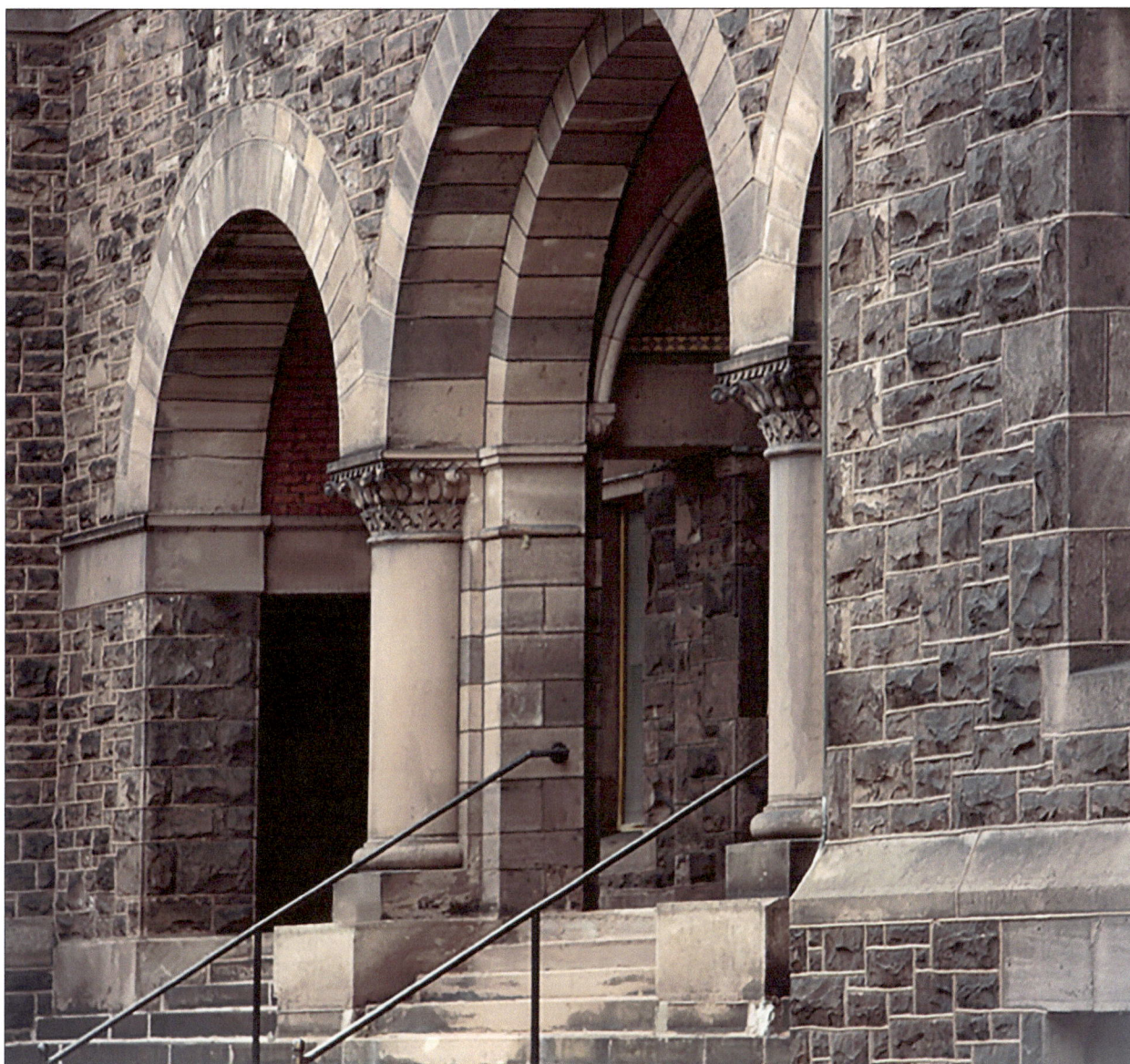

Then you can come to that hundredth, what I call "a live-wire witness," and the dam breaks. This is not a factor of a goofy witness. (Believe me, I can tell those.) It's an individual with experience at a site, an interest in the curious, and a good memory. This is someone doing your research for you. You just have to be lucky enough to meet them.

I came across one of those after a tour I'd led in East Aurora in the summer of 2013. The witness was a stonemason with a Buffalo company, a man of, I'd say, 50. In the summer of 2011 his crew was called in with other contractors to buttress some of the buildings at the Richardson Complex. He reported two experiences of his own.

One came in one of those subways. A light source was behind him, and he knew he was otherwise alone. He saw a shadow-form moving fifty feet ahead of him. He ran out as fast as he could.

He also confirmed one of the storied sound effects: the spontaneous, miraculous laughter of children. Other crews reported hearing it inside the building. He was the only one to have heard it outdoors, and he heard it twice in the same basic spot, on the south (Forest Avenue) side of the Complex. Once was as he drove up to those two towers for the first time, his window down. The sound was so vivid that he got out and looked for the source. No humans of any age were within laughing-range.

A sub-contractor our witness knew was working alone on

the third floor with a radio turned to 97-Rock on a modest volume. He left to get some cigarettes. When he came back, his radio had been tuned to some oldie-music station... and cranked! The odds that a mortal joker had done it seem slim.

The most dramatic event was reported to our friend by a plumber working on the second floor of a ward with occasional gaps in floors and ceilings. He resigned himself to doing his job–and watching his step. As he worked he listened to music on an i-Pod that suddenly shut down. He reached for his cell phone to give a bit of light and found it, too, inoperative, as if an electrical dampener was in effect. Something made him look above toward a yawning space in the ceiling. The face of an old woman peered curiously down at him. Pale and breathless, he made it back to his supervisors, begging to be transferred off the job. He vowed never to go back.

———

I interviewed a man in 2024 about his experience at the Asylum. He was in his twenties that afternoon in June, 1983, and visiting friends who had been students at Buffalo State College, which is walking distance from the old Asylum. All had heard that "there were ghosts in there," and one knew of a basement window that had been left unlocked. The four set out for an adventure.

They found the entrance and slithered and shimmied their way in, bent on touring the west wing. A series of windows gave them the light they had. The four came to a large subterranean space that had been abandoned with the abruptness one might expect of passengers fleeing the Titanic. It reminded them of a storage shed that had flooded, undergone many winters, and then dried–though this one, said my witness, "looked like a house of horrors." One decrepit antique he recalled was a metal brace, a combination fence and helmet, that could have fit around a human head like a medieval torture-device. Another contraption was a table with Frankensteinian electrodes.

The four milled about testily, touching nothing. They noticed closed doors around them as if smaller rooms waited behind them. There was also an open hallway.

Five minutes after they entered the wards a door somewhere slammed and sent two of them dashing back for their window. One stayed with my witness, and the pair observed a shadow-figure starting to approach them from the corridor. The third intruder made tracks. My witness stood. The form, he recalls today, may not have been walking. It may have been manifesting, and expanding, getting broader and taller. At one point, though, he decided it was best for him to get out as well. He made it back to his point of access and out. Whatever he had seen did not follow him–or else it was invisible in the brightness and clear air.

Except for the time of day–afternoon–and the abruptness of the incident, the tale is similar to many I've heard about the site. Those wards are wonder-zones.

What is unusual is that my witness has gone on to become a celebrated mystic and teacher in the Buffalo area. He himself clears houses and faces what others presume to be the supernatural. His conclusion today is that the apparition in the basement, whatever it was, was trying to use his own energy and that of his friends to enter our world. He avoids applying terms like "evil" or "vampire" to the source of the experience. He reflects upon what he could have learned if he had stood his ground. A message may have waited. Maybe something was ready to teach him about the realms beyond this. He is not surprised that at that point in his life he fled. He is only half-sorry about it today.

———

That 1997 book in which the Richardson does not appear has done remarkably well. "Shadows" is still in print after 27 years, which is something for a regional book. Today, I consider it a beginner book, not poorly written or designed, but early in my understanding. Every one of its chapters could have been a book of the same length.

I do not mean to scare anyone from visiting or staying at the Richardson. The Complex is a playground for the imagination, as if some force about it causes people on those rare occasions to see, hear, and sense things that they may not anywhere else. This is not, to me, a site of fear. It's one of wonder. And intrigue. And secrets waiting discovery.

4

So Would I Nurse the Dreamer of Dreams

Louis Henry Sullivan (1856-1924)

The Prudential/Guaranty Building (1894-95)

28 Church Street, Buffalo

It is much to be regretted, however common the case is, that men who have talents which fit them for peculiar purposes should almost invariably be under the influence of an untoward disposition.

George Washington

It is the pervading law of all things organic and inorganic, of all things physical and metaphysical, of all things human, and all things super-human, of all true manifestations of the head, of the heart, of the soul, that the life is recognizable in its expression, that form ever follows function. This is the law.

Louis Sullivan

Acknowledged today as the middle member of "the Holy Trinity of American architects," Louis Sullivan (1856-1924) was born in Boston of an Irish father and a Swiss mother. He came to adulthood in an era of artistic influences that included "The Celtic Revival" (or "-Twilight"), and the spirit of the Gael was never far from him. Sometimes called, "The Father of Modernism," he had a tendency to pick up epithets. Buffalo is lucky to have had him.

His father Patrick Sullivan was a dancing teacher who may have had a fondness for the poteen. I'm not sure how much of an influence he was in his gifted son's early life. Son Louis was one of those rare people who knows their gift young. He graduated high school early and aced a series of exams that let him skip his first two years at the Massachusetts Institute of Technology. He was 16 when he started—and MIT is no pushover.

However, the man in charge of architecture, William Ware, was a disciple of Richard Morris Hunt and hence a devout classicist. Hunt, a notable Freemason, designed the base of the Statue of Liberty. How the volatile Sullivan must have gritted his teeth drafting the Doric, Ionic, and Corinthian stylings he thought "mechanical and inane." He also called them, "stultified," and "lacking in common sense and feeling."

In a year he was in Philadelphia, working for Frank Furness. The Depression of 1873 dried up Furness's business, and Sullivan had to scramble. The Father of Modernism had some of the worst luck when it came to economic ups and downs.

A power of rebuilding was going on in Chicago after that gigantic fire (1871). Sullivan went to work there in 1873 for William LeBaron Jenney, often credited with the first steel frame building.

In a year Sullivan was in Paris at the École des Beaux-Arts. Sullivan disliked the classical traditions, but he learned them. They were in his psyche.

Back in Chicago, Sullivan started as a draftsman for the firm of Joseph S. Johnston and John Edelman. His talent must have showed. In 1879 Dankmar Adler (1844-1900) hired him, and in a year he was a partner. This was the best period of Sullivan's career.

The brilliant can be impatient with the merely good–and Sullivan could be easier to admire than to like. It was in Chicago, though, that he crossed paths with the ever-tempestuous Frank Lloyd Wright, then a young draftsman for the firm. Sullivan was a mentor to Wright, who revered

him even after their inevitable schism.

The World's Columbian Exposition came to town in 1893. Also known as the Chicago World's Fair, it was a temporary fairyland, a fantasy-city like Buffalo's Pan-Am of 1901. In charge of the general theme was Chicagoan Daniel Burnham, a significant power-broker in the architectural community. Prominent designers from all over the nation were in on the planning stages for the Exposition. So was Sullivan, and he was outraged. To him, Burnham groveled before the snobby classicists of the East Coast, and the Exposition went old school. "It set American architecture back a hundred years," said Sullivan. He deigned to do an arch, the famed Golden Doorway, for the Transportation Building, but his clash with Burnham couldn't have made him any new friends in his field. Before long Sullivan could have used any friend he could get.

I told you about Sullivan's luck with economic cycles. The Panic of 1893 hit Adler and Sullivan hard, and their partnership dissolved. Buffalo's Guaranty Building was their last major project.

Adler had been the dealmaker of the team, and the man Wright would come to call, *Der Leiber Meister –*

"Dear Master"–was less suited to running his own operation. His twenty-year decline was not helped by his own alcoholism. Married but separated, he died in a Chicago hotel room on April 14, 1924–broke and alone, but for, presumably, John Barleycorn, a steady but uncritical friend.

"So would I nurse the dreamer of dreams," wrote Sullivan once, "for in him nature broods while the race slumbers." As with old NFL players, I wish someone was looking out for our fine artists.

———

Sullivan was an inspiration to the group of Chicago architects who have come to be known as "the Prairie School." In the words of Wright, the most famous Prairie architect, Prairie-style houses are "married to the ground." Meant to blend in with the flat, open landscape of the American West, they go wide, not up. Buffalo's Darwin Martin House is a good example.

That hardly squares with skyscrapers, and why those aficionados took Sullivan as a spirit-guide is a question. It must have to do with Sullivan's intricate and abstract concept of "Organic Architecture." As I gather it, it's a virtually mystical theory in which a building's form merges with its purpose, the materials needed to make it, and its human and natural environment. Like Richardson–who influenced Sullivan– thought of it, the interior and exterior of a building must be in simpatico.

As Sullivan himself once wrote, organic architecture meant evoking "the initiating pressure of a living force and a resultant structure or mechanism whereby such

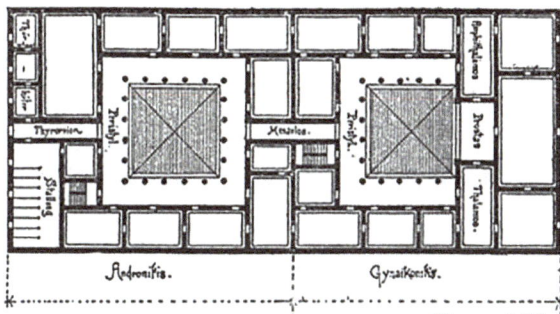

Figure: 107

invisible force is made manifest and operative." How you go about measuring the success of any such attempt is another question, yet it seems as though Sullivan expected it to run like mathematics. He was frustrated by his contemporaries for whom these principles were not so obvious.

Figure: 108

The mantra most often associated with Sullivan–"Form follows function"–is actually an old one, first attributed to Marcus Vitruvius Pollio (c. 70 BC–c. 15 BC), most commonly remembered as simply *Vitruvius*. Vitruvius' *De Architectura* is the one text on architecture that survives from antiquity, and it's a Bible, at least a beginner's manual, to many architects. "Firmitas, utilitas, venustas…"–strength, utility, and beauty–were "the Vitruvian triad" of architecture."

Figure: 106

Any disciple of Vitruvius was designing buildings of a mystical bent. Vitruvius, you remember, was a big fan of the octagonal form we'll encounter a number of times in these pages. But you can see why neoclassicism could set Sullivan off. As good as it might be for eventual ghost stories, putting a mathematically-true Greek temple in a contemporary city seemed a total mismatch.

Sullivan was one of our architects who wrote a good bit about what he did and thought. As admired as he is, his abstract theories have often unvisualizable goals. His mind was unimaginably gifted for ornamentation. Sullivan is one of the few people of his own lifetime whom Frank Lloyd Wright–not proverbial for flattery– acknowledged as an influence.

Three days before his death, Sullivan passed his autobiography to Wright with an unsteady hand. I wonder if Wright addressed him as *Lieber Meister*. He surely called him so after.

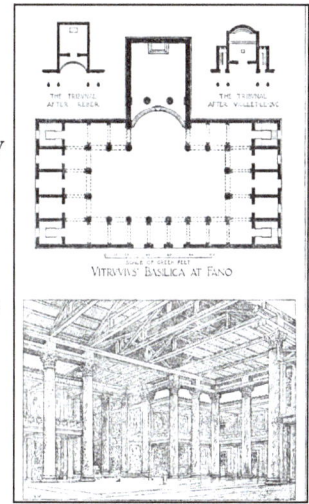

Like so many of Sullivan's buildings, the Guaranty's sheer existence has been perilous. It's undergone a couple lamentable periods of rehab and many of its loveliest original features were in witness-protection. Covered up.

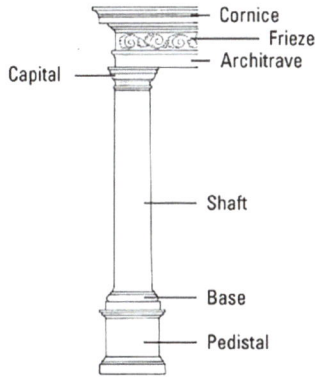

Cornice
Frieze
Architrave
Capital
Shaft
Base
Pedistal

Despite being recognized as a masterpiece in Europe as early as the 1940s, in 1977 it was threatened with demolition by an out-of-town developer. I think only the high-speed endeavors of local preservationists, a with-it judge, and late Senator Daniel Patrick Moynihan (1927-2003) may have saved it for our city. It was restored in the 1980s and was one of Buffalo's first National Historic Landmarks. Also one of our treasures, the Guaranty is world-famous for two basic reasons.

The first is that it's an early skyscraper, one of the first ever made. Its thirteen stories made it for the day the tallest building in Buffalo. That deserves a little discussion.

As American cities grew in population, you had to build up. Historically, there were two limitations on height. One was the simple matter of vertical transportation. Building heights were limited by the number of stairs you could get people to tread. That was solved in the 1860s with the invention of the elevator.

A more serious problem was the structural system, which limited building heights by the number of stones or bricks that could be stacked on top of one another. For most of history you couldn't get a building to go over three stories without having crazy-thick walls. The base couldn't support the weight above it. It didn't matter if your material was wood or stone. A new factor came along: steel.

While steel—a harder, more serviceable alloy of iron and carbon—had been known since 1800 BC and in wide use for tools and weapons by a thousand years later, its production was low-key. By 1890, steel was being mass produced, and it permitted a strong, slender, flexible

skeleton that could support many floors.

The next challenge was to make a tall blocky building look good. Louis Sullivan had the answer. In fact, he set the basic form of the American skyscraper: tall, proud, and soaring. He borrowed from earlier styles, even classical, which is ideal for a pillar-like building. The

Guaranty is an example. Look at that cornice at the top. I envision it as being made to gesture to a Greek column.

Yet Sullivan's democratic philosophies were all there within it. Its three components, base, shaft, and capital, represented the practical divisions of the human community within it. ("Form follows function," again.)

The base of the Guaranty, the first two floors, were aimed at being public space. They were to be open to the community quite freely. The elaborate cornice and round oculus (eye) windows thirteen stories over Court Street makes the capital. That was to be management's offices. Multiple, uniform office areas make up the central column, floors three through twelve, where everybody else worked. Ah, the workers always get the shaft, don't they?

It might surprise the newcomer to realize how serious ornamentation was to several of Buffalo's occult architects. Sullivan is the first of them, and one of the few whose components—simple building-parts like cornices and panels—are considered individual works of art that are worthy of being mounted in museums. This is the second reason for the fame of the Prudential/Guaranty. In that regard, it's a giant canvas, and not a classical one at all.

Even people who know little about symbolism sense that the geometric and richly botanical forms used in the Guaranty's terracotta—Latin for "burnt earth"—sheathing must mean something. Most of the designs on Sullivan's skyscraper seem derived from American nature forms and inspired in style by the Irish *Book of Kells*, that medieval work of Celtic/Christian illumination.

We have seen that any expression of occultism in the

design of a building–or the practice of it within!–will contribute to the likelihood that it someday gathers ghost stories. Expressions of occultism might include what people put on the outside of the building and on the walls and fixtures all through it.

The main motif at the Guaranty seems to be a sort of oval seed-pod, but there are a lot of nurturing vines here, too, that Sullivan could have used to suggest humanity's capacity for spiritual and creative growth–the flowering into new life. There are also winding forms interpreted to represent caterpillars, which we know are destined to morph into winged creatures, a metaphor for ascension if there ever is one. Reminiscent of interwoven Celtic imagery, they all imply a belief in a next stage coming. ("What the caterpillar calls the end of the world, the master calls a butterfly," wrote Richard Bach.) Like them, in the motif, the human being expands into Spirit when the old form is detached. This theme of growth, evolution, ascension, and rebirth is very Masonic, too, if not Rosicrucian and Theosophical.

In Sullivan's day mysticism and alternative spirituality–i. e., occultism–were rampant in the arts. "The Celtic Revival" (or, "-Twilight") was another cousin of the Arts & Crafts Movement known for its easy flow into mystical disciplines like Theosophy and Rosicrucianism. The Guaranty's Celtic-like imagery reminds me of the dreamy, mixed-motif work of "the Glasgow Four," a Scottish crew centered around artist-architect Charles Rennie Mackintosh (1868-1928) and his wife Margaret McDonald (1864-1933). They were nicknamed, "The Four," and even, "the Spook School" for their spectral figures and designs.

I wondered if Sullivan might have used the Golden Section in his Buffalo masterpiece. I got a look at what appear to be scale diagrams for the building and set the form of the Golden Rectangle atop the front facade. It fits. I didn't expect that, much less for it to be that direct. Next I got hold of a similar drawing of one of the levels, which one would presume to be the footprint of the entire building. It looks like it makes a pair of Golden Rectangles beside each other on the long side. This can't be accidental. Surely there is more of this patterning to be found here.

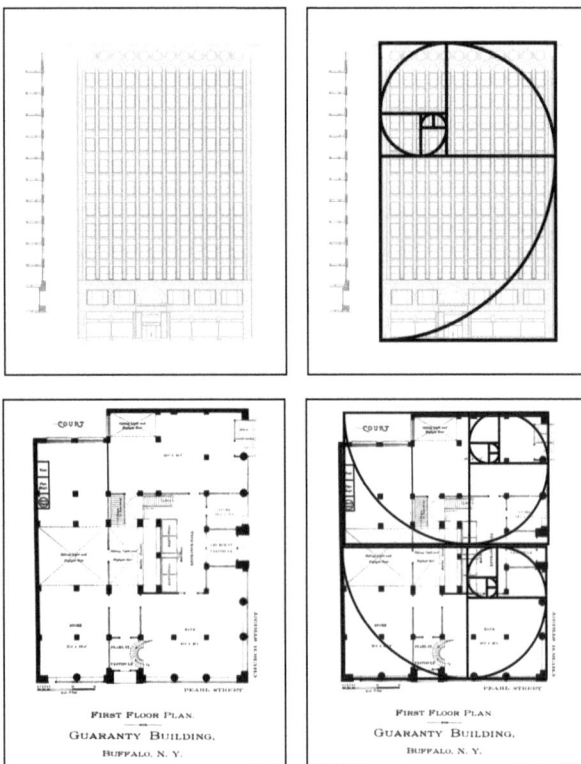

Figure: 117

In a survey of any allegedly haunted building, I find it a vital step to identify precise spots of reported experiences. Sometimes there's a pattern to be found.

Sullivan's masterpiece made a mark on quite a few people who spent time in it, and I interviewed a number of them in 2005 and 2006. Most of the EHE ("exceptional human experience") they reported fell into a pair of zones. One is the two lowest levels, the basement and first floor which, I'm told, is often open to the public.

Not all big haunts have a single prominent haunter. At the Guaranty, people seem to have settled on one. Most of them call him, "Orville." (For others he's "Oliver.") He's described as a gent in a bowler hat and other Gay 90's attire. He's been seen around the two lower levels.

One good witness was a former security guard. It started in late 2003 when the firm he worked for bought the Guaranty. One of the older guards, a holdover from the earlier uses of the building, asked him if he knew about "the Guaranty Ghost." He talked about hearing voices on vacant floors. He mentioned feelings of being watched as he did his rounds. Sometimes he felt a sudden gust of air like the passing of an invisible being. Tenants reported lights or faucets operating themselves. This is no ghost, really, no apparition. This is SPOTUK. Still, that can be all it takes to get a building the reputation of being haunted. At the Guaranty, there's a lot more.

My witness was part of the best encounter he had to retell. It started with a bit of screaming.

A server at the first floor sandwich shop rushed up to him to report a man in the women's rest room. Dressed "a little strange," he was standing in the shadows, then he was gone as if he'd disappeared. He showed again in the mirror before her as she washed her hands, as if standing behind her.

Two men went with her to investigate. No intruder was found. Yet our witness went to the spot at which the ghost had first been seen, and, on impulse, put his hand on the wall near it. The spot was ice cold.

The experiencer described the man she'd seen–I don't think I'd say, "gentleman" if he gets his jollies in ladies' rooms. He was around 5'10," with an odd beard and an antique uniform and hat. One of the old-timers heard the story and showed everyone a picture of one of the old elevator operators. The witness said it was a match.

Orville/Oliver is not the Guaranty's only ghost. Guards report hearing of a distracted woman in the lowest level. They search but never find her. A strange man–not necessarily the familiar Orville/Oliver–passed a woman working late one night, waved, and kept going. His

surprised observer checked with the guard on duty. She was advised that no one else was in the building.

The middle sections of the Guaranty seem less active. On August 1, 2006–Lammas/ Lughnasa Day for the old Celts–two construction workers on the 7th floor witnessed a door shut itself as if the Invisible Man had a need for privacy behind it. Curious, they approached it and heard women conversing. None were within sight. I suspect the next sound they heard was that of their own feet making rapid tracks.

The elevators seem to operate themselves, too, at the Guaranty, which brings us to the other major focus

Figure: 118

of the EHE, the top floor, the thirteenth. Sometimes the elevators end up there when passengers are hoping to reach another floor. Sometimes the button is pushed from that thirteenth floor, and doors open on empty space. The fact that it happens here bears a little examination.

To some world cultures, the number thirteen is neutral, if not positive, as in Asia and some Mesoamerican cultures. In most of the West, the number thirteen seems cursed. It's been said that 80% of American buildings don't give a floor that number for that reason. Why, in that more-superstitious age, did they top a building with thirteen levels? By crowning his skyscraper with that floor, Sullivan seems actually to have flouted it.

Why, at the start, might thirteen be a trigger?

There's a mystical code attached to simple numbers in many cultures. This is numerology. In most Western numerology, the number 12 is considered a nearly "perfect" number, mixing as it does the female three and the masculine four. (Squaring circles and joining opposites were ideals some of the Western mystery-schools.) The addition of the extra one seems to tip a balance. Both Judas Iscariot and the Scandinavian trickster Loki were the extra guests at pivotal dinners set for a dozen. It was on a Friday the 13th (1307) that doom fell upon the Knights Templar and sent shock waves throughout Christendom.

For the influential Gnostics, the number thirteen is special. The Gnostics were a loose association of philosophers who influenced early Christianity. They had an active number-symbolism in which thirteen was actually blessed. In Gnosticism and related forms of mystical insight, the number thirteen represents the power of the numinous, the mystical, and the indefinite, associated as it is with the lunar cycle of the year and hence female nature. There are thirteen full- or new moons in every calendar year.

What's the point of anyone emphasizing the number thirteen? It might be an expression of sympathy with the underground wisdom of the West. It wouldn't have been unique among the artists of the fin de siècle.

It's conjectured that Gnostic philosophy and imagery has been perpetuated by occult groups behind the scenes

Figure: 119

PRUDENTIAL

GUARANTY

of history–like the Freemasons alleged to have designed so much formative American symbolism. Look at the Great Seal of the United States and see how many thirteens you count: letters, berries, arrows, reeds... A version of it is on the back of the dollar bill. Thirteen rays, incidentally, are on the sunburst-flag of the City of Buffalo–and thirteen five-pointed stars.

Why did the Gnostics go underground?

The early Christians found many Gnostic ideas to be challenging, being so similar to their own in some respects but muddying the waters in others. The early Church, in fact, tried to stomp them out. It was as vicious as a fight between siblings. Never forget that Europe's last Crusade was against itself. The Albigensian campaign in the Languedoc region of France was bent on wiping out the Cathar Heresy, the last open vestiges of Gnostic Christianity. ("Kill them all," ordered the Abbot Amalric. "Let God sort them out.") It didn't go that well for the other indigenous -isms of Europe, either, including all forms of paganism. The Romans and the Church that came from Rome saw to that beat-down. I don't think the extent to which Europe was affected by the loss of its native religious heritage has been fully appreciated.

This, too, though, could be a clue. Gnostic ideas and imagery have been interesting to a long line of mystics and artists. Sullivan's emphasis of the thirteen here at the Guaranty could suggest that he had been exposed to Gnostic ideas. It could also be coincidental.

It seems as if Sullivan's mysticism may have been personal and not just a matter of executing old formulas. Newark, OH, has a complex of ancient earthworks. They're on the World Heritage list of sacred sites, and when Sullivan designed his wonderful and highly ornamented bank in that city, he was reported to be fascinated by them. People saw him every evening strolling among these monuments, evidently communing deeply. For Sullivan, these ancient expressions of a lost, mysterious culture were living glyphs into which you could walk and just... *space*.

———

"Urban Renewal" is a metaphor for the noxious postwar era of systematized architectural and hence cultural destruction. The favored style of its vernacular replacements might be likened to the futuristic space-bases on the 50s science fiction films most ridiculed by *Mystery Science Theater 5000*.

Too many of Sullivan's glorious and intricate works have been demolished for buildings that served the economic interests of a few while depriving a community of a lot. A crew of preservationists activated themselves to do what they could around the nation. By the 1970s growing public concern resulted in many of Sullivan's buildings being saved, often at last minute.

One of Sullivan's most ardent defenders was Chicago's Richard Stanley Nickel (1928–1972), a Polish-American photographer and guerrilla preservationist. ("Great architecture has only two natural enemies," said Nickel. "Water and stupid men.") Nickel organized protests and led risky expeditions into doomed buildings to rescue chunks of the magnificent ornamentation for which Sullivan was mostly responsible. Some photos of Nickel feature him perched like a gargoyle at the edge of a ruin, chiseling off some piece of mineralline wonder to be preserved.

On Thursday, April 13, 1972, Nickel took things too far on one of these midnight raids. He was attempting to pry some ornamental wonder out of Sullivan's condemned Stock Exchange building when a floor above him collapsed, dropping him with it. That's taking one for the team. I wonder if it's significant that the day was another 13th. At least it wasn't a Friday.

Figure: 121

5

The Cross Lorraine

Andrew Jackson Warner (1833-1910)
Old County Hall (1876)
92 Franklin St, Buffalo

Five architects, in my impression, dominate the haunted profile of Rochester. Four of them are part of father-and-son teams: the Searles, Henry (1809-1892) and Henry Robinson (1836-1882); and the Warners, Andrew J. (1833-1910) and J. Foster (1859-1937). Then there's the art critic, psychic, and socialite–you got that right–Claude Bragdon (1866-1946).

An aura of mystical thought coats the careers of our Rochester five, and the study of their influences takes you down conspiratorial rabbit holes. We should again be cautious. A man or woman can have–or be asserted to have–an exposure to something that does not become a compelling motive for a life's work.

The Searles to me are the most intriguing. In their quarter-century Valley span they designed some of the Genesee region's most sublime Greek Revival buildings, some I suspect still unattributed. (In the first half of the 19th century, the Genesee Valley wasn't as interested in either architecture or record-keeping as it would be soon after.) The Searles personify the extent to which some of these architects were steeped in Masonry and related mysticism. Henry Robinson Searle, for instance, contributed a heavily Egyptianate

Figure: 123

design that narrowly missed becoming the Washington Monument we see today–and a postcard for the Masons.

The Warners' influence on the Rochester skyline was almost a century long. They were a lot more classical than some of the figures we'll see in this book. The father was a prominent Freemason, and it's hard to believe the son could have escaped exposure to the Craft. One of my favorite monumental haunts on the North American continent, the Greek Revival Ontario County Courthouse in Canandaigua, NY (1858), was designed by the Searles and then expanded by one of the Warners. Talk about a train-wreck of human history and drama on that site–a succession of jails and courthouses, the Treaty of Canandaigua, the William Morgan affair, the Susan B. Anthony trial…! And a flock of ghosts.

The average person probably doesn't get the crossover between architecture and philosophy, but it's quite significant. Claude Bragdon, the fifth of the Rochester crew, was affiliated to some extent with Elbert Hubbard's Roycroft, and his falling-

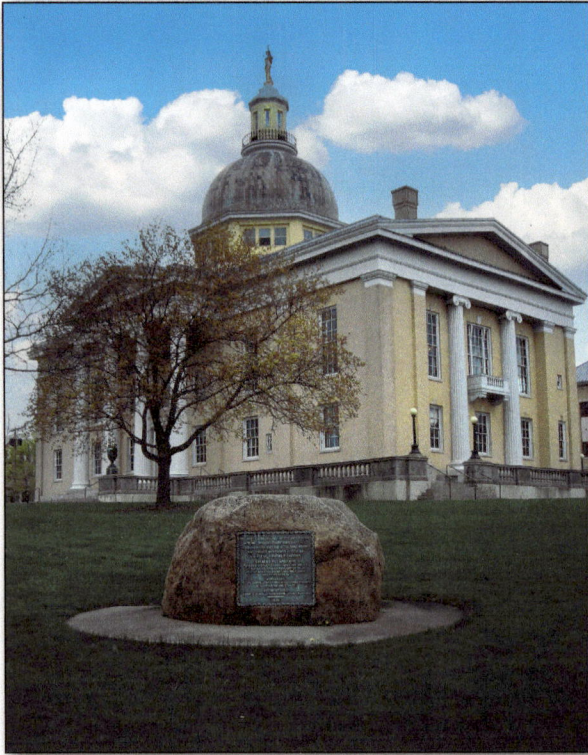
Figure: 124

"Projective ornamentation" and something called "the hypercube" were aspects of Bragdon's abstract theories. He was surely visualizing in a way few of us can follow.

But it's the Warner father to whom we turn, and for his work with one of Buffalo's grandest buildings.

———

As high as was his profile in "the Flower City," A. J. Warner (1833-1910) kept a remarkably low one in other regards. The grandson of a Revolutionary warrior, he was born in New Haven, CT. As a young man he came to Rochester to work as a draftsman for his uncle Merwin Austin and not long after established his own practice. In 1855 Warner married Catherine Pardee Foster (1834–1921). The pair had two sons, including the architect J. Foster.

Warner was a prominent Rochester Freemason. He might have been expected to use that springboard into finance or politics, but he seems to have been content with his family, his practice, and his Prince Street home. Another of Rochester's illustrious forever-denizens, he dreams today beneath the sward of Mount Hope Cemetery.

While the architect himself described Old County Hall's styling as "Norman," others call it "High Victorian Romanesque" or "Norman Romanesque." It's certainly big and castle-like.

That tower is one of Old County Hall's most prominent features. Sculptor Giovanni F. Sala intended its four

out there could quite well have been political. (While both men could have been Theosophists, Hubbard was only a situational liberal.) Bragdon's quasi-Spiritualist beliefs came out in his autobiography *More Lives than One* (1938). Like Wright, Bragdon got his start within the atmosphere of the Arts & Crafts Movement. Though not as influential as Sullivan and Wright–possibly because he surfed in their wake–he was of their ilk in viewing architecture as something that could influence society. He was big on ornamentation, too–quite Sullivanesque.

Figure:125

Figure:126

Figure:127

Figure:128

prominent goddesses to represent four cardinal virtues for the city: Commerce, Agriculture, Justice, and the Mechanical Arts. Looking out as they do from the tower's corners, they don't face the compass directions. They face the cross-quarter points. You can tell Justice, if you can get up there, by her sword and shield. She representing the mechanized arts holds a wreath and a tool, seemingly a mallet. Lady Commerce holds a caduceus, Hermes/Mercury's familiar winged-staff-with-coiled-snakes. Lady Agriculture nestles a sheaf of wheat.

———

You know how a grenade has a "kill radius"? With some of the most significant reputedly haunted sites, you get the sense that there's a folkloric influence like a "blast-zone" around them. With really heavy sites like Stonehenge or big ones like battlefields, the storytelling and paranormal reports wake outward, as if the site itself is a nucleus. Niagara Square in Buffalo has that effect. Old County Hall is not, I would think, within its radiance. Still, if it isn't haunted, it ought to be.

The haunts that interest me most tend to be layered with drama, eventfulness, and curiosity. I talk a lot about these "train wreck" sites that center cycles of coincidence and drama. Sandwiched between Delaware Avenue and Franklin Street, Old County Hall surely fits.

I don't know anything about the site's significance before the whites arrived. The block on which Old County Hall rests, though, has an energetic past. At this corner, Franklin and Eagle, Dr. Cyrenius Chapin surrendered Buffalo on the dreadful night of the city's burning. The structure lies atop the Franklin Square Cemetery, one of

the first burying grounds in the city, where many War of 1812 officers were interred, including the Seneca war-chief Farmer's Brother, laid to rest with full military honors in March, 1815. Sarah St. John was the last tenant in 1836, the year her husband Samuel Wilkinson became mayor of Buffalo. Adding to the mix, the graveyard–all 1,158 occupants, theoretically–was removed to Forest Lawn in 1850. No one suspects there are no stragglers–or parts of them. Adding to the morbid tone, a gallows did once stand on the building's north side. Doubtless its grim work left a psychic residue, at least if you believe such things are possible. All these factors are commonly associated with the outbreak and persistence of folklore.

———

I've played around with the best overhead photos I could get of Old County Hall and find it likely that, accounting for shadow-form, the overall footprint is that of the Golden Section. From there, one might conclude that the form and its other spins could be layered all through it in subtle ways. I do not push that as a conclusion. I haven't

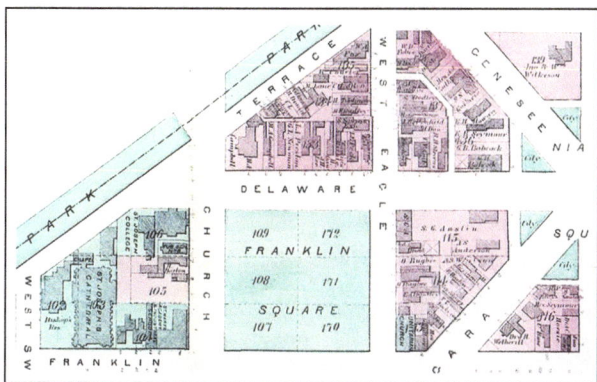

Figure:130

had any luck getting hold of the original drawings, and the site is so big and packed-in that the photos I've seen are not true to its geometry. Even the overheads have a slant.

There could be symbolism in the building's shape. The footprint of the structure is more or less that of a double-barred cross, often called the Cross Lorraine. There are mundane interpretations for the form, but it is also one that would set fanatics of *Holy Blood, Holy Grail* on a field day. In

Figure:131

strict shorthand, this cross was adopted in 1099 by Godefroy de Boullion, the first Christian ruler of the Kingdom of Jerusalem, which sets us instantly into the

Figure:129

conspiratorial occultism of the Middle Ages, the Crusades, the Knights Templar, Solomon's Temple… All that. That shape doesn't prove anything about Warner or whoever recruited him, but it's interesting.

The double-barred cross is also found on the Roycroft Seal, a sort of trademark found in some form on all the products of East Aurora's Roycroft enterprise, and likewise equipped with its own suggestion. I wrote about it in my first book, *Shadows of the Western Door* (1997), and I don't have much to add about it since.

The statue of George Washington on the east side of Old County Hall is one of the most overtly Masonic statues of him I've seen. It's known that Honest George was a Freemason, but so was almost any other white-guy achiever of his day. His British counterparts were, too. In fact, in some quarters the American Revolution has been interpreted as a clash between two major styles of Masonry, British Freemasonry (York Rite) and Continental (Scottish Rite).

Washington himself, though, had been a Master Mason. As President, he laid the cornerstone of the U.S. Capitol building in a Masonic ceremony and attired in his embroidered Masonic apron. That apron, incidentally, had

been a gift from Marquis de Lafayette, another Revolutionary war hero and Freemason. Lafayette toured the Niagara Frontier in the summer of 1825 a few months before the opening of the Erie Canal.

Figure:133

As you regard the bronze statue set here in 1976, please notice the distinctive Masonic features: the square and compass ornament (with the sun) on the apron ("the lambskin"); the Bible; the gavel of justice or, maybe, the Mason's mallet; and one of the mythic pillars of Solomon's Temple, either Jachin or Boaz, but probably Jachin as it's by the right hand.

The Croatian sculptor Joseph Turkalj (1924-2007) executed this statue in time for its dedication in 1976. A specialist in religious statues and bas-relief, Turkalj (sometimes, Turkaly) was known to consult with his clients before developing the vision that led to his finished works. It would be fun to know who coached him up for this job outside Old County Hall. Somebody made sure

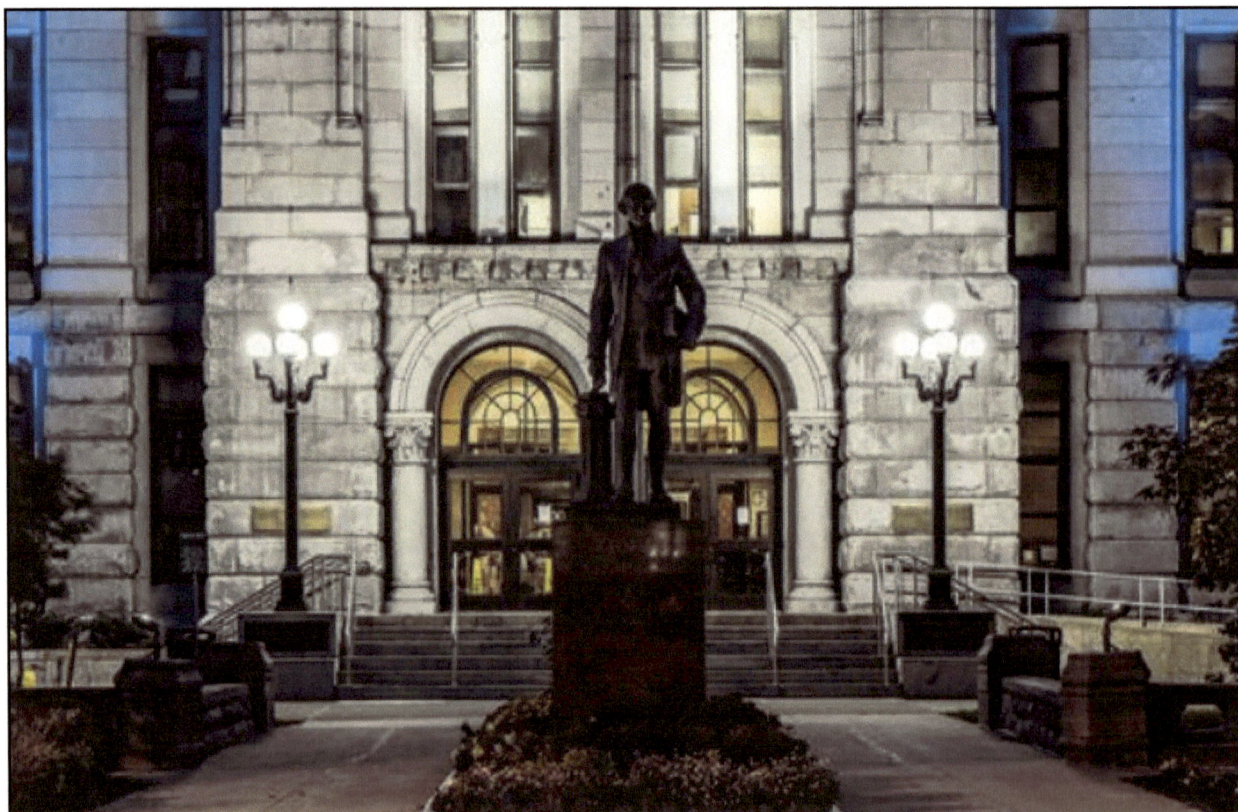

Figure:132

to emphasize the Masonic connections at the founding of the nation, as well as to Buffalo and its great courthouse. I've been told that there is only one other statue in the world of George Washington in his Masonic regalia–in Alexandria, VA, home of the lodge he founded. Why is there one in Buffalo? Here?

———

There are some curiosities at Old County Hall, and some of them relate to timing.

As we all should know, the nation's ceremonial birth is on the date it declared independence–July 4, 1776. It was on July 4, 1876, that Old County Hall was dedicated in a grand ceremony. That statue of Honest George was dedicated here on July 4, 1976.

A plaque marks the spot where President William McKinley lay in state in the lobby of Old County Hall in September, 1901. A wake of intrigue, including hauntings,

Figure:135

surrounds his ill-fated Buffalo visit. The shooting that led to his death directly followed his visit to the allegedly cursed site along the Niagara, the Devil's Hole. It was said that French explorer René-Robert Cavelier, Sieur de La Salle, could not survive its influence,

either, after his own visit in 1679. The day of McKinley's death, September 15, was the anniversary of the famous ambush-massacre (1763) that made the Hole proverbial.

The site of McKinley's shooting by the anarchist Leon Czolgosz was the Temple of Music, one of the Pan-Am's seasonal wonder-buildings. While Czolgosz met his end in the electric chair at Auburn Correctional Facility and not the gallows in the shadow of Old County Hall, he was indeed tried here, and en route to at least one of his court visits he was led by the body of the much-admired man he'd sent to glory.

———

The cathedralesque courthouse has psychic reports in layers. Let me summarize.

As I often say, any American building with a steeple, a tower, or a cupola will tend to get ghost stories, and the stories will often center around that feature. That tower is indeed a focus at Old County Hall. Workers have long dreaded it. They report hearing persistent and unexplained sounds when working on it, as if it's the energy-generator some mystics might expect it to be. It creaks and ripples like a giant animal twitching in its sleep.

The site collects indefinite apparitions and eye-corner images. Only rarely do they seem connected to identifiable people or events, including the 1901 trial of McKinley's assassin or more-recently late lawmen. Witnesses have spotted a pale well-dressed corpse on a faint table in the lobby where the late President rested in state. Incomplete apparitions in the basement could indeed be the shades of cannon-mangled war victims buried at about this depth.

The second level is another zone. I've heard reports of psychic sound effects, including phantom voices, all over the building. I've heard of manifesting ghostly faces and incompletely-forming human apparitions–the jagged torso of an old-time cop, for instance. Some employees have requested not to work there after dark.

In 2006 a security guard told me of the occasional stampede up from the lower levels of the north wing among people waiting for appointments. The only thing I could get out of anyone is that people reported ghastly, incomplete forms, sometimes in a virtual parade as if a courtroom had just let out, sometimes in a dance of death as if a cemetery of the war-wounded had decided to parade itself. In the 1990s the procession set running one young woman who was completely deaf.

A cop told me in 2006 that a captain on overnight security duty was so sure he heard people that he called in a team to search. The K-9 crew were all over the building due to these psychic voices. They found nothing, of course.

As recently as 2023 a cop was moonlighting as the night watchman on what he thought was an unoccupied building. He was called by someone from a nearby site about a light on and, seemingly, a moving human form in a second level office. He found a light unaccountably on, but no intruder. He was another who requested no more overnight duty.

Figure:136

some curse on the city's fortunes. But I don't finger the

———

In 1974, the tower's sixteen-foot, four-ton granite statues needed work, and all four were removed from County Hall. Lady Agriculture, who had originally been facing southeast over most of Erie County's farmland, must have been the last removed, because that once-a-century crane had been left before her former place. She, however, needed extra repair time. The contractors were anxious to get going and, rather than move that cumbersome crane just to keep the statues in their intended places, simply set one of the ready three, in this case Lady Commerce, into her corner. When Ms. Agriculture was up and running, she ended up in Lady Commerce's rightful space, overlooking Delaware Avenue–a funny view for agriculture. (Try growing anything on that bustling lane.) The contractors surely thought nobody would notice. They were about right, except that David Rock, an architectural history docent with Buffalo Tours, uncovered the mixup–and a clever *Buffalo News* reporter, Stephen T. Watson, got wind of it.

Mr. Rock tracked down Edward Umiker, Erie County's former public works commissioner, then 85. Umiker had been "very, very upset" when he found that the goddess-forms were not in their intended locations. He knew we'd be stuck with it that way a long time.

Only time can tell whether the statue-switcheroo signals

switch. Our problems started long before it. I'd even vote to shuffle the other statues and see what happens. It can't be a boatload worse than some of the other moves we've made.

———

Coincidences and history set us some more surprises here, some grim. The dedication ceremony for Old County Hall was held on July 4, 1876–the 100-year anniversary of the Nation's founding. It should have been a joyous birthday for the United States and a big day for Buffalo. Yet a hush went through the throng as news by telegraph was delivered–in Washington DC and here in Buffalo–of the United States military's worst battlefield loss to First Nations forces. It was George Armstrong

Figure:137

Opposite Page - Figure:138

6

The Note Unheard

George Dietel (1876-1974) and John Wade (1893-1990)
Buffalo City Hall (1931)
65 Niagara Square, Buffalo, NY 14202

Even the style of the monument isn't settled. I've heard "Art Deco," "Eclectic Classicism," and "American Modernism" bandied about. One of its designers, John Wade, referred to it alternately as "Americanesque" or even, "Babylonian." I guess it does have those stairstep-sides near the top of the tower that remind us of the Middle Eastern ziggurat. They do that with Mesoamerican pyramids, too, and many speculate about a Mayan-Revival influence. Art Deco indeed incorporated world- and Native American influences. No one argues that Buffalo's City Hall is one of the masterworks of civic architecture in any American city—and a profound, mysterious building.

A Buffalo boy all the way, George J. Dietel graduated from Canisius High School and Canisius College. As an adult, he lived on Humboldt Parkway in a house that was miraculously spared in Robert Moses' genius plan to burrow an expressway through thriving neighborhoods and an Olmsted Park. That Moses–blunt, determined, and irresistible–reminds me of one of the titanic sand-worms in the Dune-cycle.

You'd think Dietel's biography would be splashed all over the internet in architectural circles as well as historic ones. He was a big man in Buffalo and not just with architects. He may have had a quiet life, and he seems not to have done much work outside of the city. It was as if this community was world enough for him. As wrote onetime Buffalonian F. Scott Fitzgerald, "Life is best looked at through a single window." I get it. I like to travel, but I like living here.

Apart from being a partner in the architectural firm that wrought City Hall, Dietel designed Catholic churches in the Buffalo area, as well as St. Mary of the Angels Home and the first addition to Sisters Hospital. A longtime member of the National Architects Society, Dietel was well more than a detached building-artist. People thought enough of his capability to make him a director of both a bank, the Lincoln National, and a cemetery, Mt. Calvary, in Cheektowaga, where all mortal of him today rests. George Dietel passed from us in the Brothers of Mercy Home in Clarence, survived by nieces and a nephew but no named children. I couldn't find any pictures of him to show you, so maybe this makes another statement of the proverbial modesty of the figure of the architect.

———

I don't know enough about Mr. Dietel to tell you he had interests in occult architecture. I see only one hint: his association with a couple societies. Dietel was a fourth degree Knight of

Columbus and a 50-year member of the Knights of St. John (a Catholic outfit sort of like the Freemasons). Both are thought to be more fraternal than mystical, but that's what the Masons say of themselves.

The original Knights of St. John were a band of crusaders who took it upon themselves to safeguard hospitals. Also called the Knights of Malta and nicknamed, "the Hospitallers," they loved that Maltese (plus-sign) Cross. They weren't stereotyped as mystics like their notorious crusader-comrades the Knights Templar, some of whose disbanded members they may have absorbed.

As with the Freemasons, there is no established line of connection between the Knights of St. John and the medieval orders they like to align themselves with. Dietel's Knights may be no more closely related to their titular forbears than the Order of British Druids. The Knights call themselves, "a Catholic fraternal organization." That's about what the Masons call themselves, too, if you subtract the religious references. Most of that's on the level. Your average Mason–like your average Knight–is no occultist. I think I would look more to Dietel's partner for any mysteries at City Hall.

———

John J. Wade (1893-1990) was born in Hoboken, NJ, into a family of artists. Wade was in grammar school when his father died, and his mother, a skilled tapestry weaver, got him a job in an architectural firm. Rather than a violation of future child-labor laws, this was a head start into a calling. Wade alternated bouts of study at the Beaux-Arts Institute of New York City and work for Henry Hornbostel and Sullivan W. Jones, who majored in the design of grand public buildings: the Oakland City Hall, the Pittsburgh City and County Buildings, and the Wilmington City Hall. Jones (1878-1955) was Wade's

mentor at the firm, and he was a good friend to have. He was an eventual New York State Architect.

Wade served in World War I, married in New York, and joined the firm of Harold Jewett Cook in the growing city of Buffalo. Even then ornamentation seems to have been his specialty. With Cook's firm he designed the Masonic Consistory on Delaware Avenue, now the auditorium and foyer of Canisius High School. The sunburst design on the ceiling of that auditorium strengthens the argument that Wade was the designer of the Common Council skylight in City Hall whose discussion is to come.

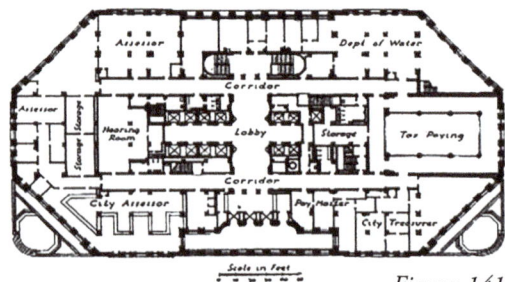

The only pictures in which Wade seems to appear are with other architects or clients. Maybe this is another sign of the obscurity of the designer. Some of them like a low profile.

In 1926 Wade formed the classic partnership with George Dietel–who sounds more like the businessman in that team. Dietel and Wade designed some local holy classics including St. Francis de Sales Church on Humboldt Parkway, St. Francis Home for the Aged in Williamsville, and the Queen of Peace Church on Genesee Street.

By 1920 it was becoming evident that Buffalo needed a new city hall. In 1926 the City Architect pitched an uninspiring design, and Wade came to the attention of the Common Council. Why not? The year before he'd written an article, "Choosing a City Hall Architect," for *The Buffalo Arts Journal*. It was a public job application. He had more practical experience with monumental projects than anybody else in town, anyway. He had been an apprentice when Sullivan Jones designed the Alfred E. Smith State Office Building in Albany, which is shaped a bit like our structure. Wade was hired in January, 1927, as the chief architect of Buffalo City Hall. He brought in his local partner.

Wade's first design was for a 25-story square tower supporting a colonnaded octagon topped with a dome of colored tiles. That's a bit like what we ended up with, but it was declined. Too much expense and too little floorspace. But people kept listening. Dietel, Wade, and Sullivan Jones were in on the final design.

On September 16, 1929, ground was broken on two lots on the west side of Niagara Square. The construction that blocked Court Street was the first interruption of Ellicott's street plan, and it may have been the first omen. (Five weeks later was "Black Thursday" that launched the Great Depression and crumbled many Buffalo fortunes.) City Hall was finished in the fall of 1931, but the dedication was saved for July 1, 1932, to fall exactly upon the City Centennial.

Figure: 145

Wade meant to make City Hall both American and uniquely local. That meant Native symbols and ornaments and representations of themes from the Niagara's past and present. "What we have tried to do," Wade tells us, "is express in stone and steel and glass something of Buffalo, just as the Greeks expressed in stone and timber their life and philosophy."

———

City Hall is not just one of Buffalo's grandest structures. It's one of the most subtle. Let's do a whole section on its potential expression of sacred shape.

We know architects put codes into the most obvious and even ponderous aspects of their buildings. Everyone regards them. Few look–or see. It shouldn't shock us if there could be a link to the earth-and-stone constructions of the distant past. They inspired several of our architects.

At a distance from any direction, City Hall's mounded

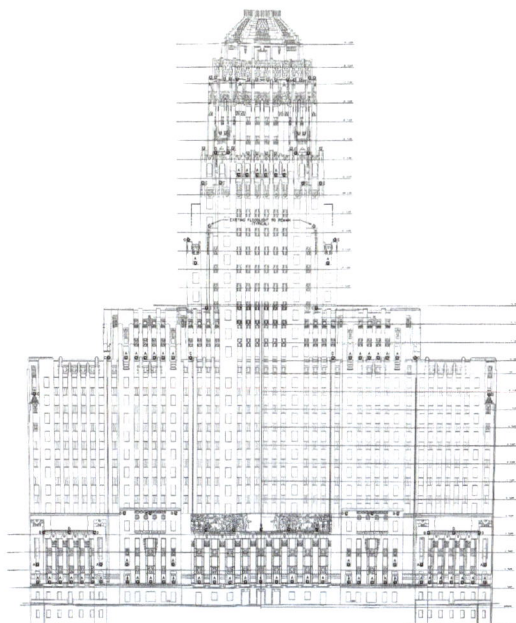

Figure: 143

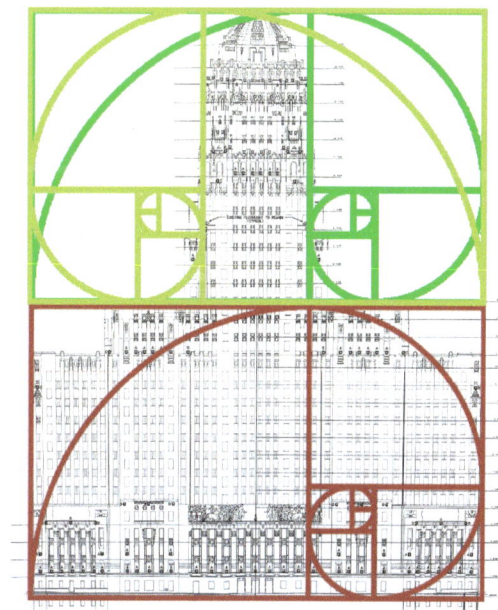

Figure: 144

THE BUFFALO CITY HALL
GEORGE F. FISK, COMMISSIONER OF PUBLIC WORKS
DIETEL & WADE AND SULLIVAN W. JONES, ARCH'T'S

NOV 12 1929
THE BUFFALO CITY HALL
GEORGE F. FISK, COMMISSIONER OF PUBLIC
DIETEL & WADE AND SULLIVAN W. JONES, A

THE BUFFALO CITY HALL

THE BUFFALO CITY HALL

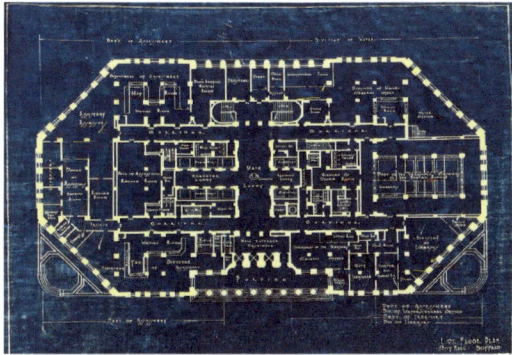

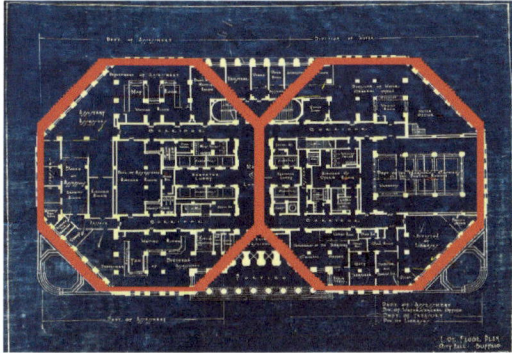

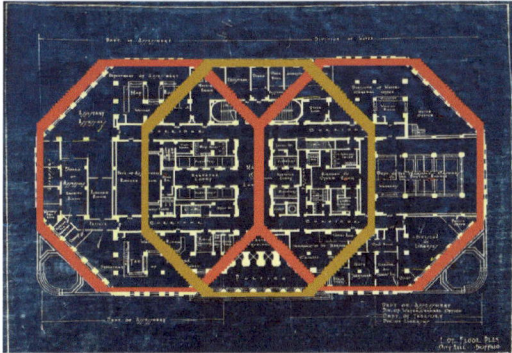

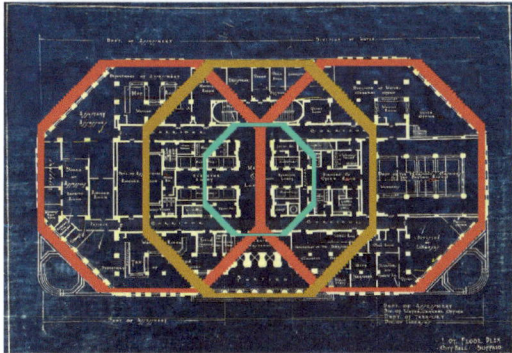

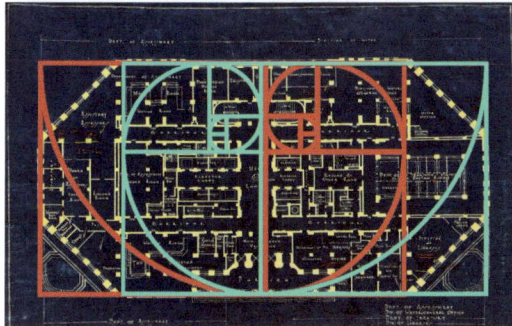

tower looms like a megalith–a menhir, one of those standing stones so common in the British Isles.

Let's look at this building from the east, from Niagara Square. Those two fifteen-story wings that lurch out from the tower give the impression of the form curving around you. Those lower, twelve-story wings further the impression. They're almost like smaller stones set in an arc about the tallest "master" stone. In my take, that perpetuates the motif of the arc. Niagara Square today is actually a circle, and the message-stones of Europe were so often set in curving forms, including unique ovals.

As with many of our urban sites, it's hard getting a photograph of a building this big that might be geometrically faithful, and I couldn't find the blueprints of the front or side. I did find a diagram that seems true to scale and took the best picture of it I could.

My impositions of the Golden Shape suggest that City Hall's profile from the major viewing angle, the east, could be meant to express shadow-form, possibly a perfect square up to the commencement of the tower levels and then two grand Golden Rectangles with its whole profile. I was, frankly, shocked to find this. I didn't think it would be that easy–or obvious.

It's interesting to note that if you duplicate the top rectangles, flip one horizontally and then superimpose it, the gap between the big squares seems to perfectly match the breadth of the tower. This has to be shadow-shape we are meant to see. Think of the great jazz riff again, this time with the delicious pauses that seem like part of the music.

City Hall's boat-shaped base–its footprint–is another wonder: an octagon, which calls us to suspect that figure as a theme for the whole. It's a likely one, too. You remember our earlier comments about the prominence of the octagon in sacred architecture. Remember also that City Hall presides over the eight-pointed Niagara Square. The Square is no true octagon, of course, nor is it even a square anymore, but through the pattern of streets that met there in the original design it makes the statement of the regular eight-sided form.

City Hall's octagon is a stretched, one, though, with an odd look of symmetry. As you'll see from our diagram made from a blueprint from the archives of City Hall itself, it appears that its length is formed by a pair of identical regular octagons resting against each other.

That octagonal tower in its core is another interesting feature. I

Opposite Page - Figure: 146 *From top to bottom Figure: 147-151*

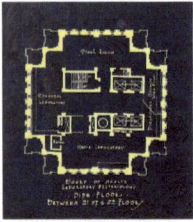
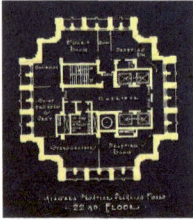

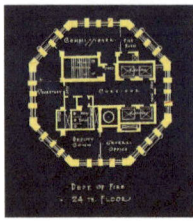

Figure: 152-155

Figure: 156

regret not to have its exact measurements, but it surely does appear as though the full form of the tower matches the length of a side of one of the big imaginary octagons.

Let's look at City Hall another way: from above. If we superimpose the Golden Rectangle over it, we find more curious matches with its internal geometry. It really does look as though the overlap makes a match with its clearly articulated semi-octagonal wings.

I wonder if City Hall could be making any other type of statement. It surely is built in a number of distinct layers. Let's look at it in cross-sections.

This long octagon you have seen at the footprint goes only a few levels up. In the next cross-section you can clearly see the Cross Lorraine that we remember from our discussion of Old County Hall.

If you did a lateral cross-section a bit higher up and for the next eight stories, you'd get a form that initially mystified me, an odd image like an F with a lengthened stem. It may be intended to express the Greek letter pi (π), that other obscure and indefinite Greek ratio. That form, too, lasts only a couple levels.

From levels thirteen to fifteen, you have a sort of U-form including the still-square tower. Other than a representation of the megalithic dolmen–the Stonehenge trilithon–I don't have a clue here.

After that, you start hitting more or less recessed levels with cut-out corners, suggesting both the square and the octagon.

With the last bank of the 32 stories we come to the eight-sided tower that gives City Hall its distinct profile. Cladded as it is in the rich and unlikely shades that ordinary paint so often takes on stucco, it is truly striking. I only wish it was nearer to the ground so more of us could savor it at close range. Here we have images of its stages.

With City Hall you could begin to consider that an even

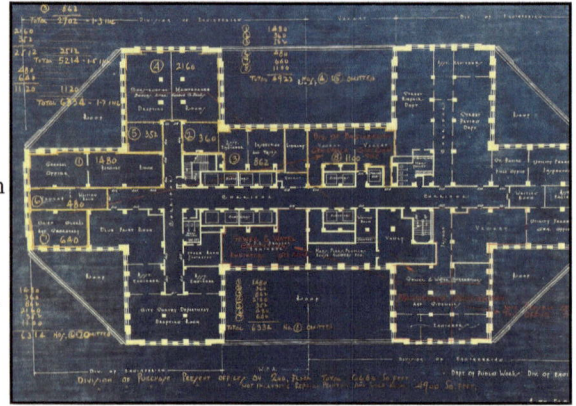

Figure: 157

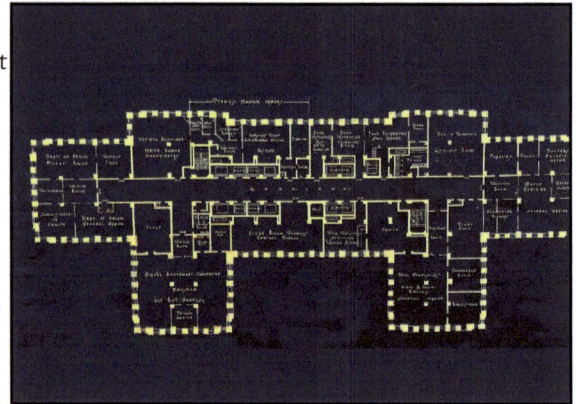

Figure: 158

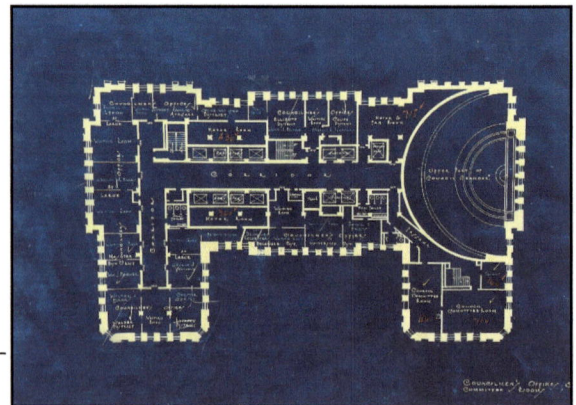

Figure: 159

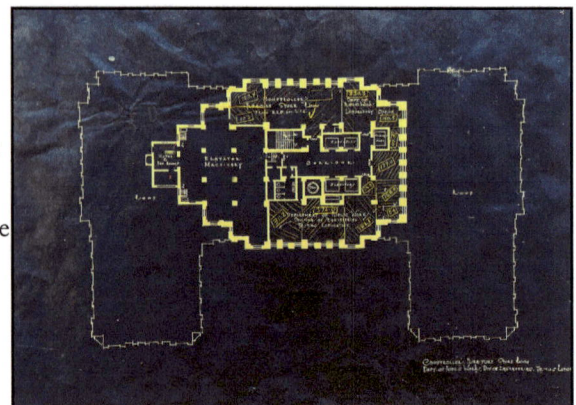

Figure: 160

alphabetic code could be presented to us. What if you imagined each of these levels as a two-dimensional glyph, a sequence of forms being arrayed like the letters of a word? First levels, a stretched octagon; second grouping, a double-barred cross; third, pi; fourth, a U; fifth, a square; sixth, a regular octagon… Would it be in a living language? Would its message even be one of words? Would it be a formula out of mathematics or physics? Would it be made to another civilization?

There could be a last, basic statement here, too. Despite the shifting forms of the layers, the building has basically five units in breadth across its long axis with its northeastern tilt: the wings at the south and north ends, the two crossing wings, and the structure of the central tower. Those five points within an eight sided footprint suggest the Golden (phi) Ratio in its shorthand form: 5:8.

It impresses me—it haunts me—to think of the other messages that could be there to be found. I hope to

inspire a more specialized scholar to take up the study.

———

We turn to City Hall's decoration. An interpretation of it would be the work of a book. I can add nothing but an occult perspective and a few ghost stories to the excellence of John Conlin's *Buffalo City Hall: American Masterpiece*. I encourage everyone to turn to it.

Figure: 162

Let's start with City Hall's murals and bas-reliefs. The paintings are dreamy, Greco-Romanized, and almost Pre-Raphaelite like the figures of Millais, Burne-Jones, or Dante Gabriel Rosetti. The reliefs seem more allegorical than occult. Most represent themes from Frontier and City history: the Iroquois Confederacy, the development of the Erie Canal, the United States'

Figure: 163

friendship with Canada, and Buffalo's frontier past and industrial present. City Hall is, after all, a Buffalo building, and its indigenous, historic, civic, and geographic significance is with it.

Yes, there are multicultural solar symbols, including the swastika in the third of our figures. You can see it in the top band on Figure 137. We talked about that image earlier. You notice that it switches directions, which the Nazi image didn't do. The Star of David appears in City Hall's iconography, too.

City Hall's exterior ornamentation is usually attributed to John Wade, who seems to have loved arcane symbolism. It's a cross-cultural quilt, with occasional Rosicrucian/Masonic overtones. There are Egyptianate lotuses and "winged sun" images. There are Judaic/Masonic "Star of David" images. There are fleur-de-lis-like forms reminiscent of undeciphered glyphs from Teotihuacan. There is a strong Native American theme in shape and coloring.

Figure: 164

In an overview, City Hall's decoration seems an expression of blessing, beaming optimism like a transmitter upon the fortunes of the region. Why would it be otherwise? Nice people who know what they are doing don't put curses onto a giant geomantic tuning fork under which the community is going to have to live–and at the power-center of the city!

Figure: 165

———

The Common Council chamber on the thirteenth floor (there we go again) is interesting. Its numerical motif seems to be sevens and thirteens. That sunburst

skylight is a true marvel, by the way. The shape of the motif is right out of alchemy and Rosicrucianism, but the imagery is native American–cornstalks, local plants, and the natural colors of the Northeastern woods. It's the radiance of the solar God with the earthly Mother overlooking and blessing the works of men. I wonder if Wade knew that almost all Native American societies were matriarchal–and their religions earth-centered.

There's plenty of symbolism, too, that isn't suggestive of occultism. Originally these pillars that surround the Chamber were meant to hold busts of famous Buffalonians, but the Council could not agree on the list. The architects suggested that the pillars be engraved with the virtues of ideal Councilmen. That the Council bought. Fidelity, Prudence, and Faithfulness are examples.

Ones you won't find are Honesty, Efficiency, and Economy. In 1931, Wade was asked why he left those seemingly important qualities out. "If the members of the city government who will occupy the new structure live up to the qualifications inscribed on the panels," Wade was quoted as saying, "the public need not worry about the city having efficiency, honesty, or economy in public service." *Economy?* Us? New York? They better get working on another pillar. Put one in Albany, too.

———

No specific ghost dominates the psychic nightlife at City Hall. Many Italian-Americans from the West Side worked on the construction, but none were left to talk to

Figure: 166

when I started my interviews in the 1990s. I've interviewed people who remembered their grandparents' stories, including talk about some spook at City Hall. Alas, none of these reminiscences are very developed. This is quite common with psychic report of any type if you don't get to the initial source. You're trying to make a pattern out of things people barely remember overhearing and weren't very interested in from the beginning.

I've heard rumors of a stately male apparition people name after one of the three Presidents who have had some connection with Buffalo: Millard Fillmore, Grover Cleveland, and William McKinley. The first two have statues here, and the third a monument. If any of them are likely to come back as haunters, Cleveland gets my vote. He hung two convicted murderers during his term as sheriff, even dropping the trapdoor with his own hand. The gallows, then–1872 and 1873–were no longer in the footprint of today's City Hall. They stood outside the Erie County Jail, then about where Buffalo Central Library is today. Think of that when you walk along that block of Broadway.

Figure: 167

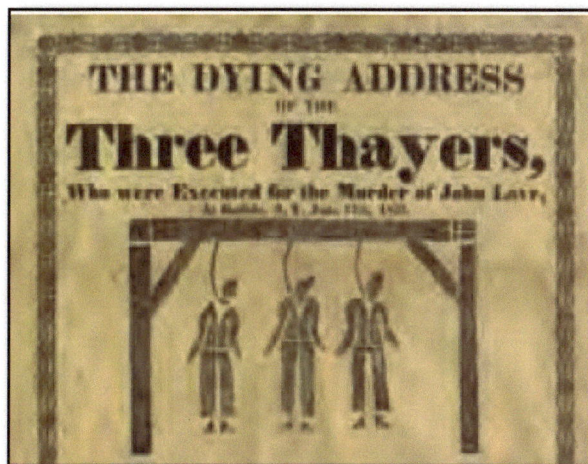

Figure: 168

Rather than an identifiable haunter–or several–the picture of City Hall seems to be that of a big EHE-zone: a realm of ambiguous phenomena. After dark, the building is a hall for mysterious sounds, footsteps, voices, and furtive shadows. None of the words people have reported hearing seem like messages. It's like the building is a big tape-recorder and video-cam, sketchily replaying past events.

———

Buffalo's last and grandest public execution was held, apparently, on a spot inside the footprint of today's City Hall. Israel, Isaac, and Nelson Thayer were three back country slackers from today's Town of Orchard Park. They were twenty-something and irreverent. They named the oxen that hauled their load of lumber to Buffalo "God Almighty" and "Jesus Christ." After each delivery they headed to the tavern. The Thayers, I mean.

In some quarters it's said that the Thayers thought they were cool characters who could get away with anything. We remember the type from high school. When the brothers fell in debt to a tenant on their farm they wondered if, instead of paying up, why not just… *Kill him?* With gun and edge, the deed was done in December, 1824. The disposal of the body was lackadaisical. (They buried the guy so shallowly that his toes were sticking out.) It would have been no more than a missing person case if the Thayers hadn't attracted attention. They managed. They tried to cash in on some of the bills people owed to their late tenant. They got caught and convicted.

When the day came, June 17, 1825, a massive crowd

had gathered at Niagara Square by the gallows outside Judge Wilkinson's house. (Some sources estimate that there were 30,000 people.) It's said that the guards were terrified of a riot and that the Thayers thought they were such studs that the mob was there to rescue them. They may even have grinned as they were led to the scaffold. Hah. People were just there to watch some string-kicking. As the truth dawned and the triple gibbet loomed, one of the brothers cut loose with an odd sound described as a sort of whistle-shriek. As, apparently, a despairing final in-joke, the other brothers—not, rightly, celebrated as wits—took it up as a call-and-answer. Back and forth it went.

It seems as if the brothers might have been making the sound of a pig, stuck or ere slaughter, reminiscent of the notorious scene from *Deliverance*. Unlike the famed and feared "Rebel Yell," we have not even the faintest recordings of anyone who'd ever heard it. Yet in a macabre, sensational stroke, the crowd picked it up. Can you imagine the sound! The whole square trilled with it. Not till the bodies were still did the eerie ululation fade.

They say that a supernatural recreation of the Thayers' piggy shrieking is still heard sometimes within City Hall. Surely it's the elevator cables! Though some have quipped that the porcine squealing is an echo of the reaction of the political class when it hears it has to cut the spending.

————

City Hall's tower is so narrow that the elevators can't go past the 25th floor. You have to climb stairs to reach the Observation Deck. Doors leading outside open onto a narrow gallery. That many-colored dome is an awesome sight up close. Awesome, too, is the panoramic view of the entire city from the core of Joseph Ellicott's radial plan.

At the time of City Hall's construction people suggested to John Wade that he might want to include some kind of security fence on the Observation Deck since it was so easy for people to jump off. Wade was known as a witty man, but he seemed to miss the point. "Are you kidding?" he may have said. "You'd have to be crazy to jump off there. I mean… Do you want to kill yourself?"

Over the years there have been too many takers. The splashiest was surely Robert Leroy Wayne Jackson, who, a week before Halloween, 1976, did a 300 foot swan-dive and skewered himself on the flagpole. I hear they had to saw through it to get him off. I also hear that a retired Buffalo Police Captain tried to sell photos of the macabre shish kebab to *Hustler* magazine–not known for its probity. Even *Hustler* wouldn't print them. The fact of the suicides may say something, though, and about power–geomantic power.

Have you ever stood close to a moving train and felt drawn into its baleful impetus? Every nerve in you ought to be pushing you away, and yet from the force and menace you feel a strange pull. Like the snake hypnotizing the bird before the strike, it calls you to lean, even though it means your doom, and just… stretch out foot or hand, and just…

City Hall reminds me of another reputed power-spot, Niagara Falls, also proverbial for suicides. Parks police have told me off the record that the public would be shocked to hear how routine the deaths are in the summer, the prime season of tourism. Every week sees at least one. Most go unreported since no one wants to encourage copycats.

But some of the people who have leaped or fallen into that liquid cyclone survive the ride and then the plunge. Many of the rescued tell us they didn't intend to commit suicide; they were there, and it was beautiful, and… Something called them to join it. With City Hall you don't get a second chance. It would be interesting to have interviewed a few of the leapers mid-leap. Clearly, this is a site of power, perhaps more than the material–and the definable.

————

For years I've been trying to figure out this structure. I know I'm still missing something. I get the sense that it's big and overt.

When his Buffalo career was done, John Wade retired to his home state of New Jersey. He left this world on the second day of 1990–at 97! It's breathtaking to realize that I could have met him. My questions could have been answered; the note could have been played! I would know it if I heard it. Maybe someone else can take up this tune. I wish I had started this study earlier.

Opposite Page - Figure: 169

7

The Song Lines

There's a story going around about the two white Australians who offered a couple of Native ones a lift back to their village. Still living by their ancestors' ways, they had never ridden in a motor vehicle. They looked to each other with apprehension as the jeep started to move. Then they did something that surprised the whites: They started to sing.

At first the back-seat pair chanted in normal tones, and the syllables and intonations of their impossibly ancient language were distinct. But when they noticed familiar landscape features drawing up to them more quickly than ever before, they sped up, mumbling crazily as if trying to keep a rhythmic, mystical carol to the pace of an uncanny new velocity. They drove themselves breathless, and before long, fell silent, looking at each other in confusion and despair like people who had let down something vital.

Anyone who spends time in the Outback has heard about them, these "Song Lines," sometimes "the Dreaming Tracks": a system of songs and chants meant to be delivered on the walking journeys the Native Australians have made across their territory for up to 50,000 years. Surely they had multiple functions. They memorialized tales, legends, and traditions that had to have been eons old. They kept their traditions alive like the Greek Homeric poets who recited vast epics by memory. They honored the land, the spirits, and the ancestors. They helped hold society and psyche together.

The trick is that every trail had its own unique song, and that, as with a grand symphony, every syllable of these performances was timed. *This* cairn represented the end of *that* poem. When *that* mountain came into sight, you commenced *this* song, and paced it to be complete at the foot. To fail to deliver the proper chants was to somehow fail in a duty to the gods, the ancestors, and possibly even the forces of the landscape. It was to weaken a cord that stretched to the ancestors as far back as they went, and to betray the children and their children to come. It was to dishonor the natural features and all the life on the earth. No wonder the two Australians looked crestfallen.

The American continents could have their analogies. We already knew the Hopewellian mounds, circles, effigies, and octagons of the Mississippi and Ohio valleys marked sacred points in time. It's new to think that they may also have been set to memorialize significant historic events and spiritual and cultural themes. They may have been story-sites. Each could have had its ritual, possibly even its festival. I've never heard it confirmed through direct sources. The monument-builders were long gone before any white ethnologists got to them. But it makes sense, and I wonder if there could be a link to our world.

Streets, sites, spooks, stories… It may seem silly to link the ephemeral ghostly folklore about our own short-lived structures to long-held traditions like those of the preindustrial world, but could such be the case, even today, in a muted form, even in Buffalo?

We call Buffalo an architectural museum which it well may be for its surviving masterworks and its representation by, in Hugh Howard's words, "the Mt. Rushmore of American architects," Richardson, Sullivan, Wright, and the earth-artist Olmsted. When you look at the treasures we've lost and keep losing, I'd almost envision us as a game preserve like those relatively tiny portions of Africa roped off for the habitat of animals who once had the run of the vast continent. As with Buffalo, the most-seasoned poachers slip by.

As this book and its second volume hope to display, when we lose one of our grand structures built to an aesthetic purpose and replace it with something whose goal is gain, we lose more than beauty–or ghost stories. We lose wonder. We lose the link to those who came before. Maybe that's why it feels like so many of us are so crazy now: We've lost connection, many of us, to our own ancestors, and we're being taught to have no respect for those of others. Maybe that's part of why so few of us value architecture enough to do something to protect it. First we have to feel why we ought to.

Photography and Illustration Index

Many of our images come from The Library of Congress, Wikipedia, and other free-use venues. Most Buffalo-area images are those of publisher Dr. Mark Donnelly, though a handful of photographs with illustration overlays are the work of author Mason Winfield.

Special notes:

1 Buffalo City Hall's skylight in the Common Council chambers is suggestive of the "illuminated" imagery of the Western mystery-schools.

3 Like the proverbial seance of the Victorian-era "performance mediums," the spontaneous poltergeist outbreak was a telekinetic madhouse.

6 One of Sig Lonegren's PR pics, truly catching his character: looking ever upward, always questing that higher level.

7 Buffalo artist Kale Johnson gives us this sketch of the dowser.

8 & 9 The Dragon Project Trust keeps for us these pictures of the legendary dowser Bill Lewis.

11 Stonehenge/Pyramid

19a & b Picture and illustration overlay of the Golden Rectangle by Mason Winfield

20 The famous Chalice Well at Glastonbury, UK, wikipedia, showing the vesica piscis

23 "The Egyptian Triangle," from a geometrical primer of Harvard University

28 The revered Alfred Watkins, rediscoverer of the ley system, and his first book

30 The Hopewell Highway, Ohio's astonishing 2000-year old ley, between Newark and Chillicothe, discovered in the 1860s and pioneered by Brad Lepper, Ph.D., and LIDAR pioneer William F. Romain. 31 "Lockyer's Triangle," AKA, "the Great Triangle of England"

32 The Ecole, Paris

34 Mt. Shasta

35 Father Alphonsus, bowed in silent communion with presences from the other world. From the biographies of St.Bonaventure University.

37 Witches frolicking at Pendle Hill, Lancashire, UK

38 & 39 Landscape symbolism in Washington, DC

40 The classic surveyor's tool, the transit

42a The bagua, the fundamental design for Feng shui

42b A vintage city map of Circleville, OH

43 The late, much-missed Steve Nelson

44 The Teotihuacan layout

45 Buffalo's Court Street ley, with added directional arrows

46 & 47 The solstice lines superimposed on the compass, then on Ellicott's 1804 map 50 Devil's Rock, Stafford, NY

51, 52, & 60 Author's pics from Saratoga Springs, NY

The portrait of the author was a yank from the author's Facebook page and then entirely the work of the publisher.

Credits

This book is in honor of the architects. Stereotyped as the most underpaid professionals and the least-remembered of artists, architects train like doctors, get paid like teachers, seldom own their work, and too often watch their dream-castles disassembled before their eyes. I've met stuffed shirts in other professions, but I have never met an architect who did not impress me–or who failed to try to help me understand something.

An architect is no John a' Dreams, no Fool on the Hill. An architect is practical. An architect is an engineer, a sculptor, and a mathematician. An architect is past that an artist–down to the handwriting! It was breathtaking to touch the blueprints of John Wade and James Johnson. Their graceful, inscrutable notations hovered like hieroglyphs on an ancient wall. Their mysterious, functional, elegant designs loomed like archetypes in the Platonic World of Forms, like constellations in the evening sky or a Hopewellian plain lighting up under a LIDAR scan!

And they can write! So many of the figures in this book and its sequel–like Wright, Sullivan, and Claude Bragdon–were philosophers and poets, whether they called themselves that or not. Buffalo is full of architects and architectural scholars who write as capably as professional writers. John Conlin, Clinton Brown, Martin Wachadlo, Chris Brown… I can't name them all. I apologize to those I missed.

The articles in this book and its sequel commenced the way they would for most of you, at least when details were generally accepted: Wikipedia, websites, and other simple bios. Then they were augmented with deeper digging, not all of which turned up ore.

My sources for the supernatural experience reported in these books are mostly interviews with witnesses, most of whom like to stay anonymous. I've been keeping files of them for decades. There were no published collections of the area's supernatural folklore before my own started appearing in the late 1990s. There are many texts on occult geometry, geology, astronomy, philosophy, and architecture as general subjects, but there were none on Buffalo's. Just about all of the occult observation in this book and its soon-to-appear sequel is winging it.

I have tried to credit those who supplied direct help in the text rather than bury mention of them in footnotes. Others who through their research, publications, insights, or other assistance helped my understanding are:

Don and Sharon Aubrecht

Chris Brown

Clinton Brown

Susan Buttaccio

Barbara A. Campagna

Steve Cichon

Sharon F. Cramer, Ph.D.

Vinny Dugo

Monica Pellegrino-Faix

Lydia Fish, Ph. D.

Austin McCracken Fox

Zoë Hill

Patrick Hoyle

Angela Keppel

Markus Kessler

Joseph Konze

Francis Kowsky

Chuck LaChiusa

Martha Mathewson

Heather Nemec

Cynthia van Ness

Lena Newman

Jack Quinan

Robert Rust

Fred Schrock

Emily Walhout

A special thanks is due to the publisher Dr. Mark Donnelly–a fine photographer, book designer, and visual artist in his own right. The only art in which he seems to lack aptitude is B. S.

THE AUTHOR

Author, researcher, storyteller, and "supernatural historian" Mason Winfield is upstate New York's premier paranormalist. Mason studied English and Classics at Denison University, earned a master's degree in British literature at Boston College, and studied poetry and fiction at SUNY Buffalo with professor emeritus and MacArthur grant recipient Irving Feldman. In his thirteen years at The Gow School (South Wales, NY) he chaired the English department, won a 50K cross-country ski marathon, and was ranked in the Buffalo, NY, area's top ten tennis players.

As a journalist, Mason writes on a range of subjects, including the War of 1812 and Celtic and First Nations folklore. He is the author or editor of nineteen books, including the upstate sensation *Shadows of the Western Door* (1997) and (with Michael Bastine) *Iroquois Supernatural* (2011), a much-praised study of the traditions of the Six Longhouse Nations. Mason's award-winning short story "The Hunters" (2000) gained honorable mention in the year's Best Fantasy & Horror. He's written a pair of occult adventures, *The Prince of the Air* (2021) and its sequel *The Elven Smith* (2024). *A Ghosthunter's Journal* (2022) details the adventures of a pair of Buffalo-based paranormal detectives. *Buffalo's Occult Architecture*, Volume 2, will be published in 2025.

Mason is a popular lecturer who's addressed audiences at the New England Antiquities Research Association, Lily Dale Assembly, the Roycroft Campus Corporation, and Larkin Square Author Series in Buffalo, NY. His talks have been sponsored by Poets & Writers, The Big Read, New York Council for the Humanities, National Endowment for the Arts, and First Night Saratoga. As a storyteller, Mason has appeared at a variety of festivals, including City of Night (Buffalo), Rochester (NY) Fringe, and Piccolo Spoleto (Charleston, SC).

Mason has been a guest on many podcast, TV, and radio programs. He designed and hosted *The Phantom Tour* (2003), a TV program/DVD on upstate New York's haunted history. He's appeared on a number of major network programs and stars in a 2006 episode of the Travel Channel program *Legend Hunters*. He appears in two more Travel Channel programs, *Mysteries at the Museum* (2018) and *Hometown Horrors* (2019).

Mason is the founder of Haunted History Ghost Walks, Inc., a company that designs tours and events with supernatural themes. Cultural, historic, and architectural preservation are vital issues to Mason, and his company has supported those causes through fund-raising events with organizations such as Lewiston Council on the Arts, the Allentown Association, The Landmark Society of Western New York, Saratoga Arts Council, Ontario County Historical Society, Wayne County History Museum, and Friends of Knox Farm State Park.

Mason is the co-founder (with Michael Bastine) of the research association Spirit Way Project, devoted to the preservation of upstate New York's supernatural and paranormal legacy. In association with Spirit Way Project, Mason is the host of a podcast series of interviews and discussions with experts in the diverse fields of the paranormal.